Garnishing
MADE EASY

Garnishing
MADE EASY

Crafting Tasty & Spectacular
Food Decorations

AMY TEXIDO, MARIANNE MULLER,
ERIK PRATSCH & HUBERT KRIEG

Sterling Publishing Co., Inc.
New York

Library of Congress Cataloging-in-Publication Data Available

2   4   6   8   10   9   7   5   3   1

Published by Sterling Publishing Co., Inc.
387 Park Avenue South, New York, NY 10016

Previously published in English under the title *Glorious Garnishes*.

Photos and text, except for the cover and the pages specified below,
© 1992 by Falken-Verlag GmbH, 6972 Niedernhausen/Ts.
English translation © 1993 by Altamont Press. Photos and text on cover and on
pages 6, 60-81, 92-93, 96-113, and 128 © 1993 by Altamont Press.

Distributed in Canada by Sterling Publishing
c/o Canadian Manda Group, 165 Dufferin Street
Toronto, Ontario, Canada M6K 3H6
Distributed in Great Britain by Chrysalis Books Group PLC
The Chrysalis Building, Bramley Road, London W10 6SP, England
Distributed in Australia by Capricorn Link (Australia) Pty. Ltd.
P.O. Box 704, Windsor, NSW 2756, Australia

Printed in China
All rights reserved

Sterling ISBN 1-4027-2007-6

Contents

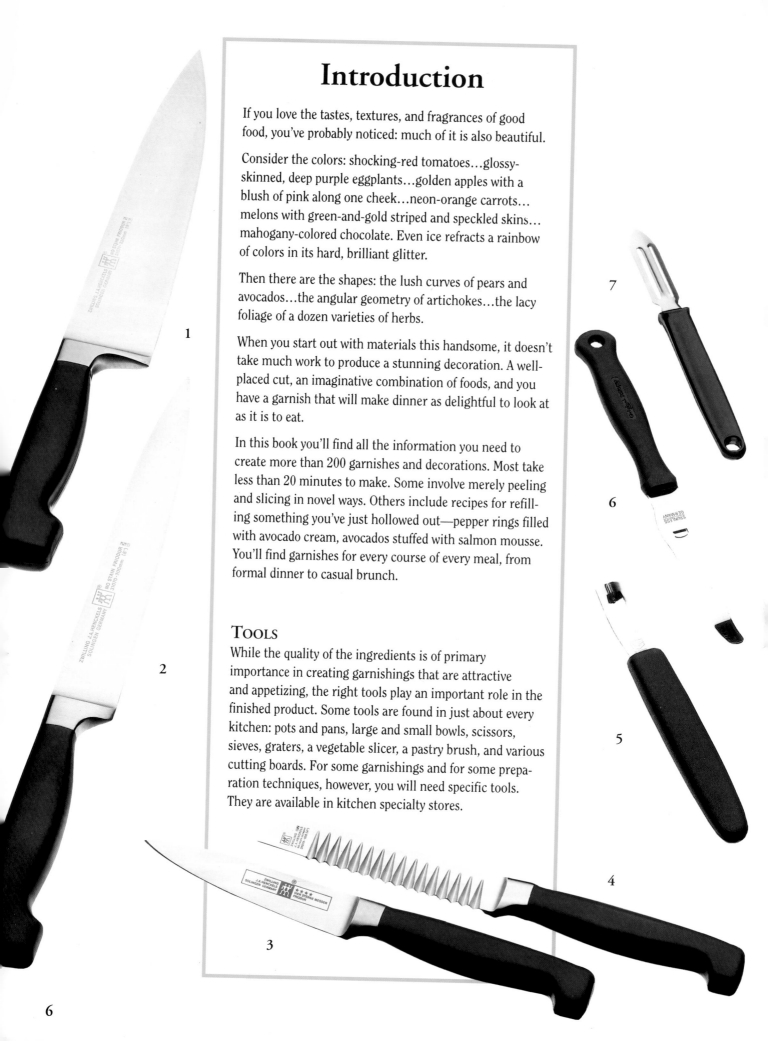

Introduction

If you love the tastes, textures, and fragrances of good food, you've probably noticed: much of it is also beautiful.

Consider the colors: shocking-red tomatoes…glossy-skinned, deep purple eggplants…golden apples with a blush of pink along one cheek…neon-orange carrots…melons with green-and-gold striped and speckled skins…mahogany-colored chocolate. Even ice refracts a rainbow of colors in its hard, brilliant glitter.

Then there are the shapes: the lush curves of pears and avocados…the angular geometry of artichokes…the lacy foliage of a dozen varieties of herbs.

When you start out with materials this handsome, it doesn't take much work to produce a stunning decoration. A well-placed cut, an imaginative combination of foods, and you have a garnish that will make dinner as delightful to look at as it is to eat.

In this book you'll find all the information you need to create more than 200 garnishes and decorations. Most take less than 20 minutes to make. Some involve merely peeling and slicing in novel ways. Others include recipes for refilling something you've just hollowed out—pepper rings filled with avocado cream, avocados stuffed with salmon mousse. You'll find garnishes for every course of every meal, from formal dinner to casual brunch.

TOOLS

While the quality of the ingredients is of primary importance in creating garnishings that are attractive and appetizing, the right tools play an important role in the finished product. Some tools are found in just about every kitchen: pots and pans, large and small bowls, scissors, sieves, graters, a vegetable slicer, a pastry brush, and various cutting boards. For some garnishings and for some preparation techniques, however, you will need specific tools. They are available in kitchen specialty stores.

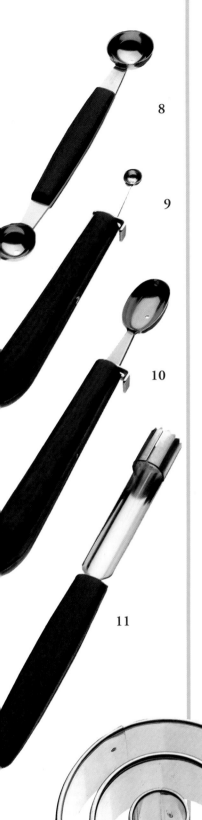

8

9

10

11

KNIVES, PEELERS, AND SPOONS

You probably have various knives. However, when you purchase new ones, make sure the blades are hardened, stainless steel. Whether wood or plastic, the handle should fit your hand comfortably. Peelers should also have stainless steel blades; otherwise, they will quickly become rusty and dull. Never use silver spoons when working with ingredients, since they might discolor fruit or vegetables. Easily breakable plastic spoons are not suitable.

Butcher knife (Figure 1) to cut up large fruits and vegetables, such as pineapples and pumpkins.

Kitchen knife or small butcher knife (Figure 2) to cut cucumbers and zucchini, divide citrus fruit, peel larger fruit, cut root and bulb vegetables, and cut up blocks of chocolate.

Peeling knife (Figure 3) to peel root and bulb vegetables, trim vegetables, clean out bell peppers, peel oranges, and make decorative cuts in fruit and vegetables.

Fluted knife (Figure 4) to make wavy, decorative cuts in, for example, carrots, cucumbers, butter, and cheese.

Peel stripper (Figure 5) to pull off strips of peel or flesh from such items as citrus fruit, cucumbers, radishes, and carrots. Unlike a zester, which removes several tiny slivers with each stroke, a stripper allows you to make one long groove at a time. The model shown has its cutting surface on the end of the tool. Other models position the cutting surface on the side, so that the tool is wielded much like a vegetable peeler.

Grapefruit knife (Figure 6) to remove the flesh from grapefruits or pineapple halves and to separate the flesh from the peel of melon wedges.

Peeler (Figure 7) to peel asparagus, celery, stone fruits, potatoes, kiwis, and avocados.

Teaspoon to remove the seeds from melon halves, the choke from artichokes, and the seeds from tomato halves.

13

12

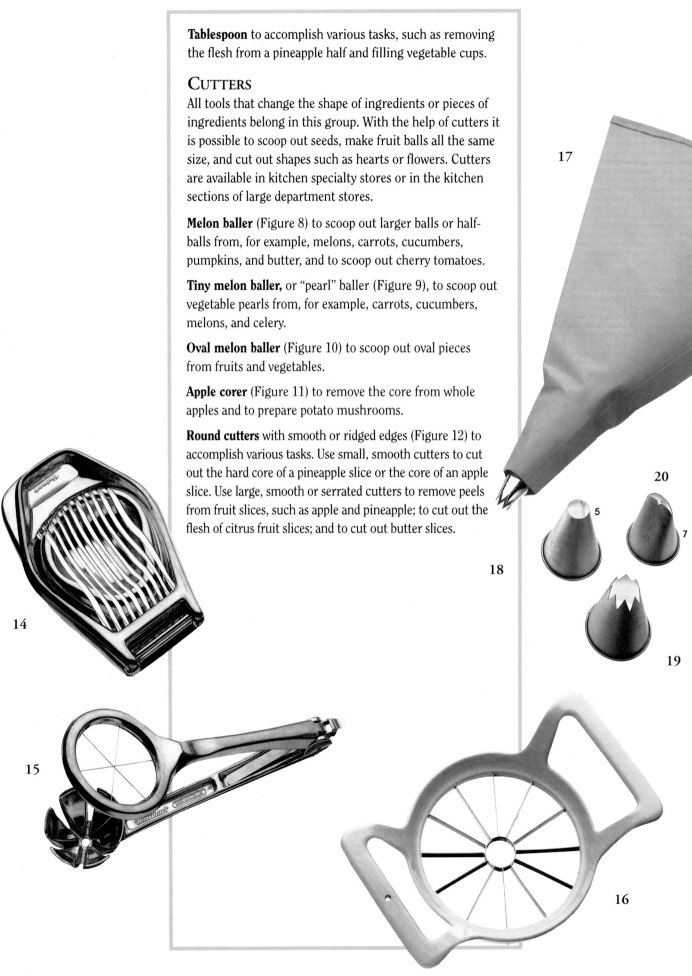

Tablespoon to accomplish various tasks, such as removing the flesh from a pineapple half and filling vegetable cups.

CUTTERS

All tools that change the shape of ingredients or pieces of ingredients belong in this group. With the help of cutters it is possible to scoop out seeds, make fruit balls all the same size, and cut out shapes such as hearts or flowers. Cutters are available in kitchen specialty stores or in the kitchen sections of large department stores.

Melon baller (Figure 8) to scoop out larger balls or half-balls from, for example, melons, carrots, cucumbers, pumpkins, and butter, and to scoop out cherry tomatoes.

Tiny melon baller, or "pearl" baller (Figure 9), to scoop out vegetable pearls from, for example, carrots, cucumbers, melons, and celery.

Oval melon baller (Figure 10) to scoop out oval pieces from fruits and vegetables.

Apple corer (Figure 11) to remove the core from whole apples and to prepare potato mushrooms.

Round cutters with smooth or ridged edges (Figure 12) to accomplish various tasks. Use small, smooth cutters to cut out the hard core of a pineapple slice or the core of an apple slice. Use large, smooth or serrated cutters to remove peels from fruit slices, such as apple and pineapple; to cut out the flesh of citrus fruit slices; and to cut out butter slices.

17

4

20

5

7

18

19

14

15

16

Small cutters in different shapes (Figure 13) to cut small motifs from bulb or root vegetable slices, bell peppers, hard-boiled egg whites, butter, marzipan, and chocolate.

SPECIALTY TOOLS

Some tools are needed for only a few garnishings, ingredients, or techniques. Others aren't actually needed at all but do make some tasks easier and more efficient.

Egg slicer (Figure 14) to divide an egg into thin slices (round or oval) and to make small egg cubes.

Egg divider (Figure 15) to cut an egg into six equal wedges.

Apple divider (Figure 16) to cut an apple in equal-sized wedges and remove the core at the same time.

Pastry bag (Figure 17) with different tips to make decorations from various materials, such as pastry dough, whipped cream or other creams, and butter. The shape produced depends on the tip. You'll need a round tip (Figure 18) for smooth shapes, a star-shaped tip (Figure 19) for ridged shapes, and a flat tip (Figure 20) for wide strips, like those in a butter rose.

Girolle (Figure 21) to make small blossoms from thinly shaved cheese.

Molds (Figure 22) for butter garnishings.

Butter cutter (Figure 23) to cut butter, scoop out butter balls, and make butter rolls.

Radish cutter (Figure 24) to make large spirals from giant radishes or ordinary zucchini.

Metal spatulas and molding woods (Figure 25) with different patterns to mold marzipan figures.

22

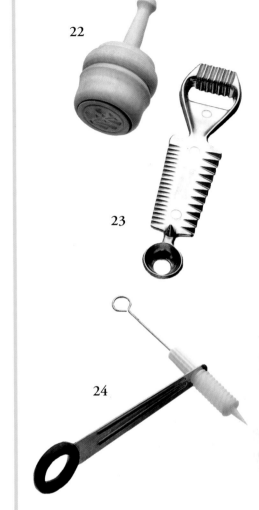

23

24

21

25

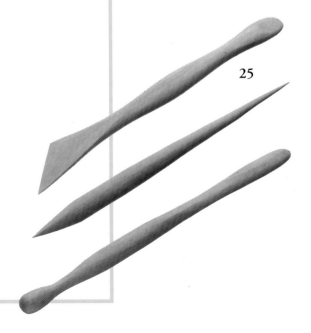

Fruiting Vegetables

ARTICHOKES

Originally from the Mediterranean region, artichokes grow on thistlelike bushes. They have green to purplish leaves and usually range from 3 to 5 inches (7 to 13 cm) in height and 5 to 18 ounces (150 to 500 g) in weight. Artichokes stay fresh for two to three weeks in the refrigerator, but they should be covered with plastic wrap so they do not dry out. The most valuable part of the vegetable is the fleshy bottom, or heart, which is excellent for stuffing or decorating. Artichokes are usually eaten cooked. Never boil them in aluminum pots; they will turn black.

AVOCADOS

Technically a fruit, the avocado is used like a vegetable. The average specimen weighs somewhere between 7 and 14 ounces (200 and 400 g). Depending on the variety, the peel is either thick or thin, smooth or rough. The color of the flesh can vary between pale yellow and light green. Avocados are harvested and sold when green and unripe. They are ripe when the peel gives slightly to pressure. When ripe, they can still be stored for about 10 days in a cool place. Scooped-out avocados are very suitable for garnishings, but slices are also frequently used. Drizzle cut avocados immediately with lemon or lime juice, since their flesh turns brown when exposed to the air. If you're using only half an avocado, leave the pit in the other half when you refrigerate it; some cooks argue that the pit slows the discoloration. When heated, avocados acquire a slightly bitter taste.

BELL PEPPERS

Bell peppers are available in various shapes and sizes and in a rainbow of colors: red, green, yellow, orange, and purple. Best- quality peppers have skin that is firm, smooth, and shiny. In the vegetable drawer of the refrigerator, peppers will keep for up to one week. Because of their thin flesh, firm texture, and bright colors, they are ideal for garnishes. They can be stuffed, sliced into strips or rings, or cut out in various shapes.

CUCUMBERS

Salad cucumbers are so universally familiar that it is not easy to determine their origin. There are many sizes and types, but the best ones have firm flesh and a small core.

Because of their texture and rich green color, they are well suited for imaginative garnishing. Cucumber pickles can also be used in many ways, as long as they are free of blemishes.

EGGPLANTS

These relatives of the tomato come from the tropics and subtropics. Eggplants regularly grow up to a foot (30 cm) in length and up to 2 pounds (1 kg) in weight. Their flesh is spongy, light-colored—almost white—and rather unappetizing when raw. Only after cooking does the eggplant develop its appealing flavor. The fruits are ripe when the peel gives slightly to pressure. They can be stored for around 10 days in the refrigerator. Eggplants are usually used raw for garnishings, either stuffed or acting as a base for skewered meats, vegetables, and fruit.

PUMPKINS

Pumpkins come in a riot of colors, sizes, and shapes, and most look highly decorative on buffets—for example, when scooped out and stuffed. A ripe pumpkin sounds slightly hollow when tapped on the outside. The flesh should be bright orange and crisp, not soft and stringy. Usually the whole pumpkin is used for garnishings.

TOMATOES

Red, pink, or yellow, huge or tiny, tomatoes are available in a multitude of guises—the small cherry or cocktail tomato, the well-known round tomato, the egg-shaped type, and the beefy, fleshy variety. The liquid content depends on the type. Not-quite-ripe tomatoes will ripen well in a warm room. Tomatoes are sensitive to cold. When stored in the refrigerator, they take on a glassy look and lose much of their taste. Because of their beautiful color and their firm flesh, they are very well suited for garnishing.

ZUCCHINI

Like many other vegetables, versatile zucchini are related to the giant pumpkin. When ripe, the flesh ranges from white to light green. The flesh is firmer in texture and less juicy than that of a cucumber. In the vegetable drawer of the refrigerator they can be stored for up to two weeks. Raw zucchini are perfect for garnishings such as stuffed turrets and boats.

CHERRY TOMATOES

Because of their delicate size, cherry tomatoes are eye-catchers by themselves on plates or platters. Larger fruits can be used for miniature baskets. For the basket, cut a lid off the top and carefully scoop out the tomato with a small melon baller (Figure 1). Use a pastry bag to fill the basket with cream.

PEELING TOMATOES

Use very firm tomatoes for this purpose, since the flesh loses its firmness when peeled. Remove the green stem, cutting out a wedge at the top. Make small crosswise incisions at the bottom. Place the tomato briefly in boiling water, then plunge it into cold water. The skin can then be peeled easily with a knife (Figure 2). For garnishings, it is possible to use peeled as well as unpeeled tomatoes.

SCOOPED-OUT TOMATOES

Scooped-out tomatoes are perfect for stuffing. First, halve an unpeeled tomato across the middle. Then scoop out the seeds, using a teaspoon or a melon baller (Figure 3). To give the tomato halves more stability, cut a slice off the round bottom (Figure 4). When a larger tomato half is needed, cut a lid off the top and then scoop out the inside as described.

Tomatoes

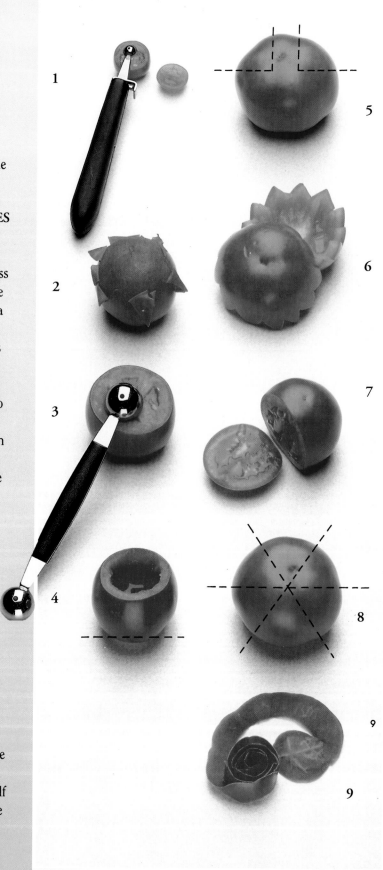

1

2

3

4

5

6

7

8

9

9

TOMATO BASKETS

Cut out two pieces at the top of a tomato (Figure 5), leaving a handle in the middle. Remove the seeds, using a teaspoon or a melon baller. Cut a slice off the bottom of the basket to make it stable. Stuff with your favorite filling.

TOMATO CORONET

Make a zigzag cut around and into the center of an unpeeled tomato, using a small knife. Then twist the two halves in opposite directions to separate them. Scoop out the halves with a teaspoon or a melon baller (Figure 6). Cut a slice off the bottom to make the coronet stable.

TOMATO SLICES

Tomato slices can be used for creating pretty patterns. Cut an unpeeled tomato into 1/2-inch (1 cm) slices (Figure 7). The end pieces are not used.

TOMATO WEDGES

Wedges can be used for arranging attractive ornaments. Cut an unpeeled tomato in half, then cut the halves in three equal-sized wedges (Figure 8).

TOMATO ROSE

Start with a firm tomato. Cut off the peel in a 1/2-inch (1 cm) wide spiral strip, using a very sharp knife. Then roll the strip into a rose, loosening the roll as the rose gets larger (Figure 9).

Tomatoes With Egg Yolk Cream

FOR 4 TOMATOES:

4 hard-boiled egg yolks
6 tablespoons soft butter
1-1/2 tablespoons cooked, finely chopped spinach
Mustard
Worcestershire sauce
Black pepper
Salt
4 medium-sized unpeeled tomatoes

PREPARATION TIME:
App. 20 min.

1. Push the egg yolks through a fine sieve into a bowl, or mash them with a fork until smooth. Drain the prepared spinach.

2. Whip the butter with an electric mixer until creamy. Stir in egg yolks and spinach, and add mustard, Worcestershire sauce, pepper, and salt to taste.

3. To serve, cut off the tops of the tomatoes and scoop out the seeds. Use a pastry bag with a star-shaped tip to fill the tomatoes with egg cream.

Tomato Halves With Shrimp Aspic

FOR 4 TOMATOES:

1 scant tablespoon (1 envelope) unflavored gelatin (or 3 sheets)
1/2 cup (120 ml) fish stock or bottled clam juice
1/2 cup (120 ml) dry white wine
Salt and pepper
3 sprigs fresh dill
4-5 oz (125 g) cocktail shrimp
4 medium-sized unpeeled tomatoes

PREPARATION TIME:
App. 20 min

1. Soak gelatin in the fish stock for 3 to 4 minutes, then heat and stir until all granules are dissolved. Add the wine and a pinch of salt and pepper. Heat but do not boil. Set aside to cool.

2. Wash and finely chop the dill. Stir into the broth together with the shrimp.

3. To serve, halve the tomatoes across the middle and scoop out the seeds. Pour the liquid shrimp filling into the tomatoes and cool in refrigerator for 2 hours, until the aspic has hardened.

Tomato Halves With Avocado Cream

FOR 4 TOMATOES:

1-1/2 teaspoons (1/2 envelope) unflavored gelatin (or 2 sheets)
1/2 avocado
1/2 teaspoon lemon juice
1/2 tablespoon medium dry sherry
1/2 teaspoon walnut oil
3-4 tablespoons whipped cream
Finely grated horseradish
Salt and pepper
4 medium-sized, unpeeled tomatoes

PREPARATION TIME:
App. 20 min.

1. Sprinkle gelatin over 1/4 cup (60 ml) cold water and set aside to soften.

2. Peel the avocado half, cube the flesh, and puree it.

3. Heat the gelatin until it dissolves completely, then stir it into the avocado puree.

4. Stir in lemon juice, sherry, and oil. Blend in the whipped cream, then add horseradish, salt, and pepper to taste.

5. To serve, cut a lid off the top of the tomatoes and scoop out the seeds (see page 12). Fill the tomatoes with avocado cream and chill for about 2 hours in the refrigerator, until the cream is hardened. Then halve the tomatoes vertically or cut them into thick slices.

TOMATO HALF WITH SHRIMP

Prepare the tomato half with shrimp aspic (see page 13). Place it on a serrated slice of cucumber with a moon-shaped piece of cucumber peel and two pepperoni rings.

TOMATO ROSE ON LEAFLETS

Place a tomato rose on several small herb leaves.

STUFFED BASKET

Use a small melon baller to carve balls of zucchini, carrots, and kohlrabi. Blanch them briefly in boiling water, along with some green peas, and toss in a vinaigrette sauce. Spoon in the vegetables, and garnish with pea pods.

STUFFED CORONET

Blanch some small cauliflower and broccoli florets, toss the vegetables with a little vinaigrette, spoon the vegetables into a coronet, and place on a slice of ham.

TOMATO ROSE ON TARTLET

Mix thin strips of iceberg lettuce with 1 teaspoon mayonnaise and place on a miniature tart shell or sturdy cracker. Place a tomato rose on top and garnish with radicchio strips.

STUFFED CHERRY TOMATO

Fill a scooped-out cherry tomato with egg yolk cream, and place it on a halved, scooped-out quail egg; cut the egg flat at the bottom for stability. Use a small melon baller to cut out a carrot ball, then blanch it and place it on top of the tomato with several herb leaves.

Tomato Half
With Shrimp Aspic

Stuffed Tomato Basket

Stuffed Coronet

Tomato Rose on Tartlet

Stuffed Cherry Tomato

Tomato Rose on Leaflets

14

Stuffed Tomato

Yellow Cherry Tomato With Olive

Tomato Flower

Tomato Blossom

Tomato Butterfly

Ornament of Tomato Slices

YELLOW CHERRY TOMATO WITH OLIVE
Place a stuffed green or black olive in a scooped-out cherry tomato. Place the tomato on a thick slice of heart of palm.

BUTTERFLY
Use two peeled tomato wedges, two chives, pea pods, olive pieces, and a pickle fan.

TOMATO BLOSSOM
Make a V-shaped incision in the peel of a tomato wedge and peel the skin off. Cover the flesh with blanched spinach.

STUFFED TOMATO
Scoop out a tomato, and fill to the top with egg yolk cream (see page 13). Cut out a wedge of the tomato and place it next to the whole tomato. Garnish with vegetable "pearls" created with a small melon baller.

TOMATO FLOWER
Use eight peeled tomato wedges and eight leaves of parsley to arrange a flower. Top the tomato wedges with olive slices and place a fluted mushroom head (see page 36) in the middle of the blossom.

ORNAMENT
Prepare the tomato with avocado cream (see page 13). Cut in 1/2-inch (1 cm) thick slices and place the slices next to each other, slightly overlapping. Top with a slice of preserved black walnut and a walnut half.

15

CLEANING BELL PEPPERS

Wash the bell pepper and cut off a lid about 1 inch (2.5 cm) from the top (Figure 1). Remove the white pith with a small knife and wash out the seeds.

BELL PEPPER CUP

Clean the bell pepper as described. If necessary, cut a slice from the bottom so the pepper will be stable (Figure 2). Be careful not to cut too much; the shell must hold the filling. Fill the cup to your liking.

Bell Peppers

BELL PEPPER BOWL

Cut the bell pepper in half lengthwise, clean it, and remove the stem (Figure 3). If necessary, cut the bottom flat. Fill to your liking.

CUTOUT BELL PEPPER

Clean bell pepper as described and cut into about 1-inch (2.5 cm) wide strips. Use small cookie cutters to cut out shapes (Figure 4). Arrange the shapes in attractive groupings.

16

Filled Pepper Rings

Pepper Crown With Rice Salad

FOR 10 BELL PEPPERS:

2/3 cup (130 g) rice
1-1/3 cups (150 g) frozen peas
1 cup (100 g) sliced mushrooms
2-1/2-ounce (75 g) slice ham
1 tablespoon walnut oil
4 tablespoons mayonnaise
Salt and pepper
Lemon juice
10 red or green bell peppers
10 walnut halves

PREPARATION TIME:
App. 40 min.

1. Cook rice for about 15 minutes, following package directions. Rinse under cold water, drain, and let cool.

2. In the meantime, prepare peas according to package instructions, leaving them slightly undercooked. Clean mushrooms with damp cloth and cube them. Also cut the ham into small cubes.

3. Mix the rice, peas, mushrooms, and ham. Stir together the walnut oil and mayonnaise; add lemon juice, salt, and pepper to taste. Add the dressing to the salad.

4. Cut off a zigzag-shaped lid from the top of the bell pepper (see Tomato Coronet, page 12). Clean and wash the pepper, cutting the bottom flat if necessary. Spoon the salad into the coronet and decorate with walnut halves. Other garnishings-might include asparagus tips, rolled-up ham slices, and fluted mushroom heads (see page 36).

FILLED PEPPER RINGS

Prepare avocado cream following the recipe on page 13. Clean two red bell peppers, fill with cream, and refrigerate for 2 hours. Then cut the pepper into 1/2-inch (1 cm) wide rings and lay them so that they overlap slightly. For decoration, place a very thin slice of smoked salmon and a sprig of dill on top of each slice.

FILLED PEPPER BOWL

Toss 2 tablespoons corn kernels and 2 tablespoons kidney beans in vinaigrette and spoon the mixture into bell pepper bowls. For decoration, use cocktail corn and peeled tomato strips.

Pepper Crown With Rice Salad

Filled Pepper Bowl

Eggplant

Artful Eggplant Hedgehog

PREPARATION TIME:
App.1/2 hour

FOR 1 HEDGEHOG:
- 2 ounces (50 g) Edam cheese
- 2 ounces (50 g) Tilsit cheese
- 2 ounces (50 g) Gruyere cheese
- 2 ounces (50 g) Emmenthaler cheese
- 6 small, thin slices salami
- 3 pickled cocktail corn
- 6 red grapes
- 6 green grapes
- 1/2 eggplant, halved lengthwise
- 6 cherry tomatoes
- 3 small pickled peppers
- 6 tangerine segments
- 6 radish coronets (see page 32)
- 6 stuffed, green olives
- Wooden picks

1. Cut all of the cheeses into 1/2-inch (1 to 2 cm) cubes. Roll salami slices into funnels.

2. Cut the cocktail corn in half crosswise. Wash grapes and cherry tomatoes.

3. Place the eggplant, flat side down, on a platter. Stick one cheese cube together with one other ingredient on a wooden pick, and pin it into the eggplant.

4. Continue picking ingredients into the eggplant, distributing them more or less evenly over the surface and aiming for a -hedgehog shape. Insert a red cherry tomato into the narrow end, for a nose.

Avocados

Avocado Slices With Smoked Salmon Cream

FOR 20 AVOCADO SLICES:

1 scant tablespoon
   (1 envelope) unflavored
   gelatin (or 4 sheets)
4 tablespoons beef broth
5 ounces (150 g) smoked
   salmon
3 tablespoons crème
   fraîche (or 2 tablespoons
   whipping cream plus
   1 tablespoon sour
   cream)
A few drops red food
   coloring
Salt and pepper
1/3 cup (80 g) cream
2 ripe avocados

PREPARATION TIME:
App. 1/2 hour

1. Sprinkle gelatin over beef broth to soften, and set aside. Soak gelatin in cold water for about 10 minutes.

2. Cut salmon into cubes and puree it together with the crème fraîche, in blender at low setting. Push the puree through a fine sieve, blend in the food coloring, and add salt and pepper to taste.

3. Heat the broth and gelatin, stirring until all granules are dissolved. Cool slightly, then add it to the salmon. Stir the cream mixture until it cools and starts to gel.

4. Whip the cream and mix in 1/4 of it, then carefully fold in the rest.

5. Cut avocados in half lengthwise and remove the seeds. Peel the halves and scoop out some of the flesh with a plastic spoon. Fill with the salmon cream, smooth the top surface, and refrigerate the avocados for 2 hours, until the cream is set.

6. To serve, cut avocado halves in wedges or slices. Garnish with cutout vegetables.

AVOCADO HALVES

With a large knife, cut lengthwise all around the avocado. Twist the avocado halves in opposite directions to separate them, and remove the seed with a knife. Squeeze some lemon or lime juice on the flesh to prevent discoloration. (If one half is not used immediately, leave the seed in it.)

AVOCADO FAN

Peel an avocado half and make comblike incisions on one side; then use your palm to press the fan so it unfolds (see Pear Fan, page 44). Place bamboo sprouts with zigzag border and cutout red bell pepper circles (see page 16) in between the fan blades.

AVOCADO ORNAMENT

Cut an unpeeled avocado half into triangle-shaped wedges (see Cucumber Wedges, page 26). Make a V-shaped incision on the narrow side of the wedge and carefully remove a triangle of peel. Arrange an ornament using the wedge together with an asparagus tip, the removed peel triangle, and a slice of peeled tomato.

AVOCADO SLICES WITH EGG YOLK CREAM

Fill an avocado with egg yolk cream (see page 13) and cut into slices.

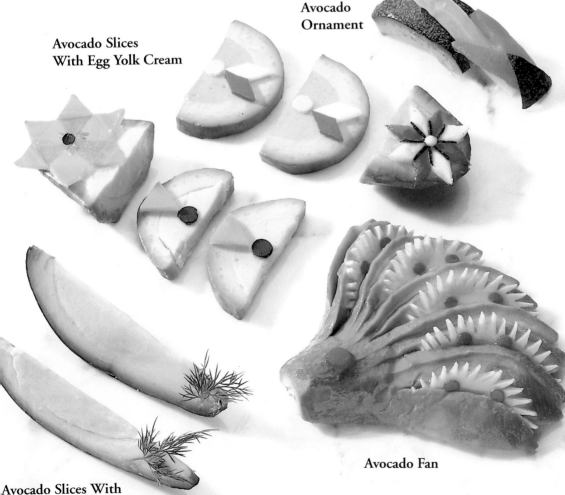

Avocado Slices With Egg Yolk Cream

Avocado Ornament

Avocado Fan

Avocado Slices With Smoked Salmon Cream

COOKING ARTICHOKES

Break off the artichoke stem on the edge of a table (Figure 1) or cut it off with a knife. Then cut the bottom flat and snip off the tips of the leaves, using kitchen shears. Tie a slice of lemon to the bottom and another to the top (Figure 2) to prevent discoloration. Boil in salted water with some lemon juice for about 25 to 45 minutes, until leaves can be removed easily. Remove the artichoke from the water and drain it head down.

ARTICHOKE HEART

Break off the stem of an uncooked artichoke, remove the hard leaves, and cut the bottom flat (Figure 3). Cut off the leaf tips so a 2-inch (5 cm) base remains, and carefully remove the choke, using a melon baller (Figure 4). Squeeze lemon juice onto the heart and cook as directed above.

ARTICHOKE BOWL

Cut the top off a boiled artichoke (Figure 5). Remove some of the inner leaves and the choke.

ARTICHOKE HEART WITH HAM MOUSSE

Prepare the ham mousse as described on the opposite page. Wash a red and a green chili pepper, cut off the tips, and remove the seeds. Use kitchen shears to make several cuts from the tip almost

Artichokes

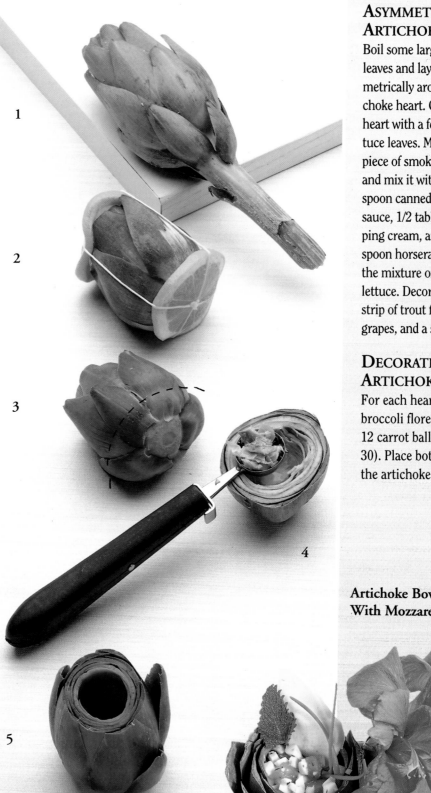

1

2

3

4

5

**Artichoke Bowl
With Mozzarella Stuffing**

to the stem and place in cold water until the "blossom" opens. Insert them into the ham puree.

ASYMMETRICAL ARTICHOKE HEART

Boil some large artichoke leaves and lay them asymmetrically around an artichoke heart. Garnish the heart with a few curly lettuce leaves. Mince a small piece of smoked trout filet and mix it with 1/2 teaspoon canned cranberry sauce, 1/2 tablespoon whipping cream, and 1/8 teaspoon horseradish; spoon the mixture on top of the lettuce. Decorate with a strip of trout filet, red grapes, and a sprig of dill.

DECORATED ARTICHOKE HEART

For each heart, blanch a broccoli floret and about 12 carrot balls (see page 30). Place both on top of the artichoke heart.

Artichoke Bowls
With Mozzarella Stuffing

FOR 4 ARTICHOKE
  BOWLS:
1 hard-boiled egg
3-1/2 ounces (100 g)
  mozzarella
1 tomato
1 tablespoon white wine
  vinegar
1/2 teaspoon lemon juice
2 tablespoons water from
  boiling artichokes
3 tablespoons olive oil
1 teaspoon chopped
  lemon
Salt and pepper
4 cooked artichoke bowls
Chives for garnish
Whole herb leaves for
  garnish
8 Indian cress blossoms or
  other edible flowers

PREPARATION TIME:
App. 1/2 hour

1. Peel the egg. Cut the egg and the mozzarella into small cubes. Peel the tomato (see page 12), halve it, remove the seeds, and cube it.

2. To make a vinaigrette, stir together the vinegar, lemon juice, artichoke water, oil, chopped lemon, and salt and pepper.

3. Mix the egg, mozzarella, and tomatoes with 2/3 of the vinaigrette.

4. To serve, spoon the stuffing into the artichoke bowls. Garnish with chives, herbs, and blossoms, and drizzle remaining vinaigrette on top.

Artichoke Heart With Ham Mousse

Artichoke Heart
With Ham Mousse

1. Sprinkle gelatin over beef broth and set aside to soften.

2. Cube the ham and puree in blender. Peel the tomato (page 12), halve it, remove the seeds, and puree it also.

3. Whip the butter creamy and blend with the ham and tomato puree. Add the crème fraîche and paprika to taste.

4. Heat the gelatin-broth mixture and stir until all granules are dissolved. Add broth to ham mixture and stir until the mixture cools.

5. When the ham mousse begins to gel, whip the whipping cream and stir it into ham mixture.

6. Use a pastry bag with a round tip to press the mousse into the artichoke hearts. Refrigerate for 2 hours or until set.

FOR 8 ARTICHOKE
  HEARTS:
1-1/2 teaspoons (1/2 envelope) unflavored gelatin
  (or 2 sheets)
2 tablespoons beef broth
1/2 pound (250 g) boiled
  ham
1 small tomato
6 tablespoons soft butter
4 tablespoons whipping
  cream or crème fraîche
Sweet paprika
1/2 cup (125 g) whipping
  cream
8 cooked artichoke hearts

PREPARATION TIME:
App. 1/2 hour

Asymmetrical Artichoke Heart

**Decorated
Artichoke Heart**

21

Pumpkins
Strawberry-Orange Salad in a Pumpkin

FOR 1 MEDIUM-SIZED PUMPKIN:

1 green bell pepper
1 red bell pepper
2 tablespoons sugar
1/4 head iceberg lettuce
1 cup (200 g) strawberries
2 oranges
1 tablespoon balsamic vinegar
Pinch English mustard powder
1 tablespoon white wine
3 tablespoons sunflower oil
2 tablespoons orange juice
1 pumpkin coronet
Mint leaves

PREPARATION TIME:
App. 1 hour

1. Preheat oven to 400° F (200° C). Halve, clean, and wash the bell peppers, and place them flat side down on a baking sheet. Bake peppers in oven until the skin blisters. Remove the peppers from the oven, briefly cover them with a damp cloth, and pull off the peel. Cut the peppers into strips. On low heat, carefully melt the sugar in a heavy pan. Add the pepper strips and stir to coat. Remove the peppers and set aside to cool.

2. Separate and wash iceberg lettuce leaves and tear them into bite-size pieces.

3. Clean, wash, and halve strawberries. Carefully peel oranges and cut them into segments (see page 56). Sprinkle the strawberries and orange segments with vinegar.

4. To make the marinade, dissolve the mustard powder in the wine. Blend in the oil and the orange juice.

5. Toss pepper strips, orange segments, strawberries, and iceberg lettuce separately in the marinade.

6. To serve, place the iceberg lettuce in the pumpkin coronet. Then add the pepper strips, the orange segments, and the strawberries in a decorative way. Garnish the salad with mint leaves.

PUMPKIN CORONET
Make a zigzag cut in the upper half of the pumpkin, cutting around and into the center with a large knife. Twist the two parts against each other to loosen, and remove the lid. Remove the seeds and stringy pulp with a large spoon. Lean the lid against the pumpkin when serving.

PUMPKIN PIGLET
Working with a slightly undercooked piece of pumpkin, carve out a large ball with an ice cream scoop and a small ball with a melon baller. Use a wooden toothpick to pin the two balls together, creating the piglet's body and head. Cut two small triangles from the pumpkin piece and fasten them to the head for ears, using half a toothpick for each ear. Pin a small round piece to the face as a snout. Press two peppercorns into the face (for eyes) and two cloves into the snout (for snout holes). For the tail, twist a thin piece of pumpkin into a spiral and fasten it to the body. Set the pig in a bed of alfalfa sprouts.

Stuffed Pumpkin

Pumpkin Piglet

ZUCCHINI BOATS

Peel the zucchini, halve them lengthwise, and cut them into pieces about 3 inches (7 cm) long. Round off the ends and cut the bottoms flat to make them stable. Scoop out the tops somewhat with a teaspoon, so the boats can hold the stuffing more securely.

ZUCCHINI ROSETTE

Flute a zucchini with a peel stripper. Pierce the zucchini lengthwise with a wooden kebab stick. Use a sharp knife to cut around and into the zucchini, cutting only as far as the kebab stick and continuing down the zucchini in one long spiral cut. Remove the stick, pull the spiral open, and lay it in a ring. (The spiral will be easier to open if placed in cold water for a few minutes.) Put a thick zucchini slice in the middle and place a tomato rose (see page 12) on top.

ZUCCHINI BLOSSOM

Halve an unpeeled zucchini lengthwise and shave off a thin slice on the cut side. Along one edge, make comblike incisions. Roll up the slice tightly and secure the uncut side with a wooden toothpick. Set it upright and pull the single petals apart.

Zucchini

Zucchini Boats With Vegetable Salad

1. Clean and wash the vegetables. Cut the carrots into 1/2-inch (1 cm) thick diagonal slices and the beans into 1-inch (3 cm) long pieces. Cut the broccoli and cauliflower into small pieces.

2. Blanch carrots, broccoli, and cauliflower for about 3 minutes, and the beans for about 2 minutes. Refresh the vegetables under cold water and drain.

3. Mix the vinegar with salt and pepper, stir in oil, and add the walnut halves. Mix the vegetable pieces with the marinade.

4. To serve, spoon the vegetable salad into the zucchini boats.

FOR 4 ZUCCHINI BOATS:

1 ounce (30 g) each carrot, broccoli florets, green beans, and cauliflower florets
1 tablespoon white wine vinegar
Salt and white pepper
2 tablespoons walnut oil
4 walnut halves
4 zucchini boats

PREPARATION TIME: App. 15 min.

Zucchini Boats With Vegetable Salad

Zucchini Rosette

Zucchini Blossom

23

Cucumbers

CUCUMBER BASKET

Cut an unpeeled cucumber crosswise into 2-inch (5 cm) long pieces. Then use a small knife to make two horizontal cuts, one from each end. Make two vertical cuts with a fluted knife (Figure 1), creating a scalloped handle. Remove the two wedges (Figure 2) and scoop out the basket with a melon baller.

CUCUMBER TURRET

Flute an unpeeled cucumber with a peel stripper (see page 7) and cut crosswise into 1-1/2-inch (4 cm) long pieces. Scoop out the turrets with a melon baller (Figure 3).

CUCUMBER CORONET

Cut an unpeeled cucumber crosswise into 3-inch (8 cm) long pieces. Make a zigzag cut around and into the center of the cucumber, and twist the halves to separate them (Figure 4).

Cucumber With Fennel Pipe

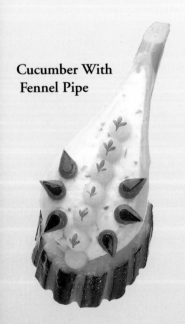

FENNEL PIPE

Place a piece of fennel on a fluted cucumber slice (Figure 5). Fill with herbed cheese spread and top with cutout pieces of bell pepper, vegetable pearls, and herbs.

CUCUMBER BOAT

Halve an unpeeled cucumber lengthwise and scoop out the flesh with a spoon. Cut the cucumber into 2-1/2 inch (6 cm) long pieces.

CUCUMBER PANICLE

Using a 2-1/2-inch (6 cm) long piece of cucumber, cut off a 1/2- inch (1-1/2 cm) thick strip down one long side. Cut the smaller cutoff side diagonally. Then make comblike diagonal incisions into the cucumber piece (Figure 6). Bend every other strip toward the middle (Figure 7).

CUCUMBER FLOWER

Cut an unpeeled cucumber lengthwise into six equal pieces and remove the seedy flesh. Cut the long pieces into about 2-1/2-inch (6 cm) long pieces with a diagonal cut on both sides. Then make diagonal, comblike incisions on one edge (Figure 8). Form rings out of the strips (Figure 9).

CUCUMBER BASKET WITH RATATOUILLE

Prepare a frozen package of ratatouille or mixed vegetables according to instructions, and spoon 1 or 2 teaspoons into the basket.

Cucumber Boats With Roquefort Cream

FOR ABOUT 10 CUCUMBER BOATS:

2 ounces (60 g) Roquefort or other blue cheese
6 tablespoons soft butter
1/2 cup (125 g) dry cottage cheese
Salt and black pepper
Sweet paprika
10 cucumber boats
3-4 stuffed green olives

PREPARATION TIME:
App. 15 min.

1. Cut the Roquefort into cubes and drain any liquid from the cottage cheese. Place in food processor, along with the butter, and process until smooth.

2. Add salt, pepper, and paprika powder to taste.

3. To serve, use a pastry bag with a round tip to squeeze the cream into the boats in three long strips. Cut the olives into slices and garnish the cream.

CUCUMBER TURRETS WITH CURRIED CREAM

For 6 towers, combine 2 tablespoons of crème fraîche or heavy cream, 1 tablespoon mayonnaise, about 1/4 teaspoon mango chutney, some apple and banana cubes, and 1/4 teaspoon curry powder. Spoon the cream into the turrets and garnish with 1 small piece of lobster meat and some blanched vegetable balls. On top place a lobster cut from eggplant, purple bell pepper, or commercial garnishing gel, and add a sprig of dill.

CUCUMBER CORONET WITH ROSE

Place 2 or 3 teaspoons of creamed cottage cheese on a cucumber coronet, and top with a tomato rose (see page 12). Garnish with dill.

STUFFED CUCUMBER PANICLE

Fill the loops of a panicle with tiny pieces of peeled tomato.

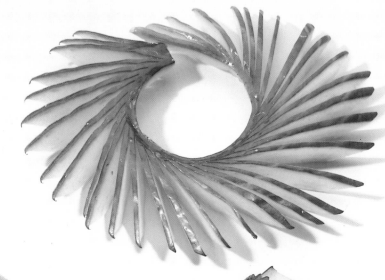

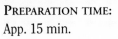

Cucumber Boats With Roquefort Cream

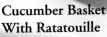

Cucumber Basket With Ratatouille

Stuffed Cucumber Panicle

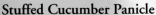

Cucumber Turrets With Curried Cream

Cucumber Crown With Rose

FLUTING A CUCUMBER

Use a peel stripper to pull strips of peel from a cucumber (Figure 1).

CUCUMBER SLICES

Cut an unpeeled or fluted cucumber crosswise into thin slices (Figure 2). For oval slices, make diagonal cuts (Figure 3). For a variation, cut the slices in half.

CUCUMBER WEDGES

Cut an unpeeled cucumber lengthwise in half and place it cut side down. Cut the cucumber into small triangles (Figure 4).

CUCUMBER BALLS

Press a melon baller into a peeled or unpeeled, firm cucumber, and carve out small balls (Figure 5).

CUCUMBER FAN

Cut a 3/4-inch (2 cm) thick cucumber slice and halve it. Place one half cut side down and make comblike incisions (Figure 6) along one edge. Pull the thin slices apart to make a fan shape (Figure 7).

Cucumbers

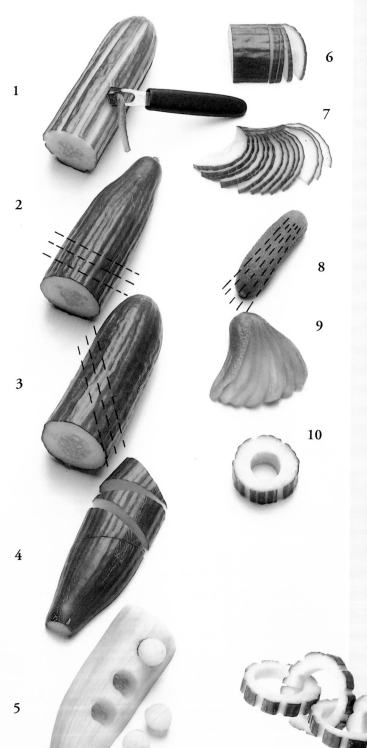

GHERKIN FAN

Cut off a thin slice on each long side of the gherkin. Then make comblike lengthwise incisions (Figure 8) and press down on the gherkin to open up the fan (Figure 9).

CUCUMBER RING

Scoop out the middle of a 1/2-inch (1 cm) thick fluted cucumber slice so that the slice has the shape of a ring (Figure 10).

CUCUMBER FISH

Peel half a bell pepper (see page 16) and cut out the shape of a fish, minus the tail. Use a cucumber fan for the tail fin. Use half a peppercorn for an eye.

Cucumber Chain

CUCUMBER CHAIN
Cut through one side of several cucumber rings and lock them into each other, forming a chain.

CUCUMBER GRAPE CLUSTER
Use equal-sized cucumber and watermelon balls to form a grape cluster. Cut shapes resembling leaves out of thick cucumber peel and place them at the top of the cluster.

CUCUMBER AND CARROT GARNISH
Use equal-sized slices of blanched carrots and unpeeled cucumber. Cut the same size triangles out of both. Then fit pieces of carrot into the cucumbers and vice versa, and arrange the ornaments in rows.

CUCUMBER RABBIT
Cut a triangle into the top of a cucumber wedge, starting at the wider edge with the tip toward the narrow edge. Then, starting from the wider side, cut underneath the peel, stopping slightly before the tip of the corner and loosening the peel from the cucumber. Remove the peel triangle. Place the cucumber in cold water until the ears made from cucumber peel stand up. Cut two small holes for the eyes and fill them with small carrot pieces.

Cucumber Grape Cluster

Cucumber and Carrot Garnish

Cucumber Rabbit

Cucumber Fish

Root Vegetables and Mushrooms

CARROTS

These colorful vegetables are available all year round. When stored with their green leaves still attached, carrots stay fresh for about one week in the vegetable drawer of the refrigerator. Larger carrots should be peeled for garnishing purposes; smaller ones need only be scraped lightly. Carrots that are used for garnishes should be straight and firm. Since they usually don't turn soft even when sitting in warm air for some time, carrots are very well suited for garnishings.

POTATOES

By now there are more than 100 varieties of potatoes, which are divided among three categories: waxy, semi-waxy, and mealy. For garnishes use the firm, waxy ones. Always use cooked or baked potatoes, since raw potatoes discolor easily and are not suitable for eating.

RED RADISHES

Because of their bright color and their crunchy texture, radishes are well liked as garnishes. Use only fresh and undamaged ones. Radishes stay fresh longer when the green leaves are cut off immediately, since they draw fluid from the bulbs, which then shrivel up.

WHITE AND BLACK RADISHES

Radishes are some of our oldest cultured plants. Some varieties grow up to 12 inches (30 cm) long and are available in white, red and black. To locate the large white or black ones, you may need to check a market that sells specialty produce or an Oriental foods store (Daikon radish is one popular variety). A fresh, white radish should be straight, crunchy, and undamaged. Store it in the vegetable compartment of the refrigerator.

MUSHROOMS

Of the many fungi that are available, the mushroom is about the only one that is suitable for garnishes, since it stays fresh for quite some time. Most widely available are the common white and brown types, both of which make good garnishes. Fresh mushrooms should have closed caps and no signs of damage. Before using, wipe them clean with a damp cloth. If you immerse them or wash them under running water, they will become spongy and water-logged.

MORELS

They are usually available fresh and dried. There are many types, but the most common is the pointed morel. Wash fresh ones thoroughly and soak dried ones in water for five hours before using. Morels have a zesty taste and are suited for stuffing.

Carrots

FLUTING CARROTS
Wash, peel, and slightly undercook a straight carrot, then run it under cold water. Use a peel stripper to pull off fine strips of flesh (Figure 1).

CARROT SLICES
Cut a peeled or a fluted, slightly undercooked carrot into slices, using a straight or fluted knife (Figure 2). For a variation, cut the slices in half and arrange them in patterns.

CUTOUT CARROTS
Use small cookie cutters to cut shapes out of cooked carrot slices (Figure 3). Cut out even smaller shapes from the inside of the slices and fill the cavities with the same motif cut from celery, kohlrabi, turnip, jicama, or another vegetable (Figure 4).

CARROT BALLS
Press a small melon baller into a peeled, uncooked carrot and twist the melon baller to remove the carrot balls (Figure 5). Slightly undercook the carrot balls.

CARROT BLOSSOM
Peel a 6-inch (15 cm) long strip from a peeled, uncooked, 3-inch (7 cm) long piece of carrot. Then lay the strip flat and make small, parallel incisions in the middle (Figure 6). Do not cut through the sides of the strip. Fold the strip lengthwise (Figure 7), roll it up from one end, and fasten the blossom with a wooden toothpick (Figure 8).

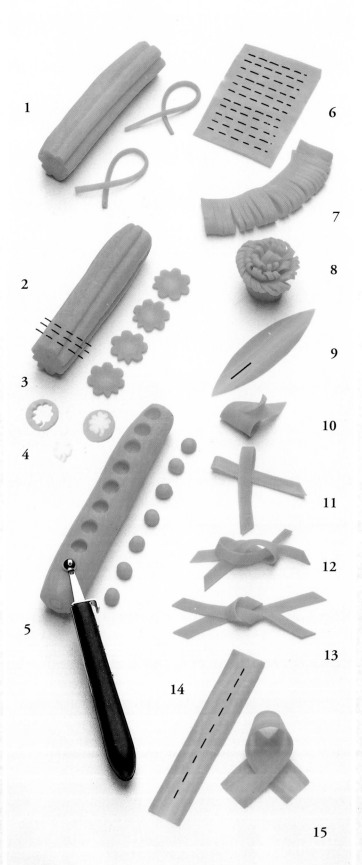

CARROT TWIST
Cut an elliptical shape out of a thin carrot strip. Make a small incision on one end (Figure 9) and pull the opposite end through the cut (Figure 10).

CARROT TIE
Blanch two very thin, long strips of carrot about 1/2 inch (1 cm) wide, refresh under cold water, and dry. Bend the strips into loops and place one inside the other (Figure 11). Hold the loops so they don't slide. Then pull the ends of the inner loop through the outer loop (Figure 12). Carefully pull the tie knot tight and cut off the ends diagonally (Figure 13).

CARROT BOW
Shave a fine strip off an uncooked, peeled carrot. Blanch it, refresh it under cold water, and dry. Make a cut along the middle of the strip without cutting through either end (Figure 14). Push one end through the cut (Figure 15). The strips will twist into spiral shapes. For a more intricate bow, pull one end through the cut twice.

CUTOUT CARROT ORNAMENT
Arrange ornaments using carrot and zucchini pieces cut into rhomboid shapes and bell pepper triangles.

MOTIF WITH CUTOUT CARROTS
Arrange a flower using chive stalks, cutout celery, cutout carrot shapes, and small celery leaves.

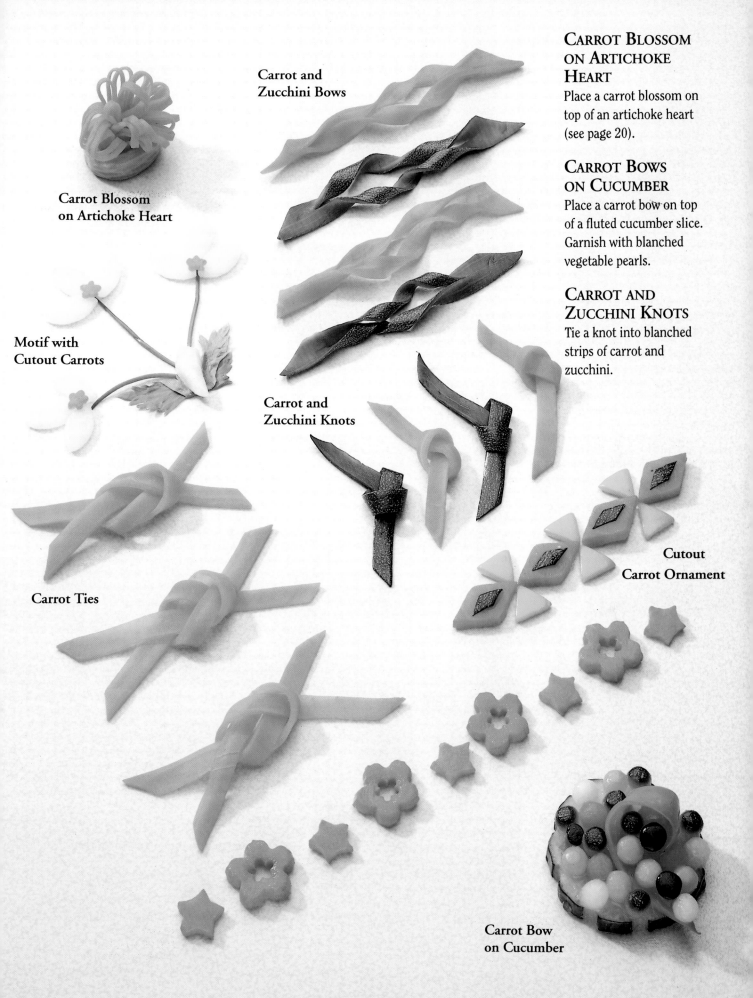

Carrot Blossom
on Artichoke Heart

Carrot and
Zucchini Bows

Motif with
Cutout Carrots

Carrot and
Zucchini Knots

Carrot Ties

Cutout
Carrot Ornament

Carrot Bow
on Cucumber

CARROT BLOSSOM ON ARTICHOKE HEART

Place a carrot blossom on top of an artichoke heart (see page 20).

CARROT BOWS ON CUCUMBER

Place a carrot bow on top of a fluted cucumber slice. Garnish with blanched vegetable pearls.

CARROT AND ZUCCHINI KNOTS

Tie a knot into blanched strips of carrot and zucchini.

31

RADISH ROSE

Make five incisions from top to bottom all around the radish. The cuts must overlap somewhat (Figure 1). Cut off the stem. Place the rose in cold water until it "blooms."

RADISH WATER LILY

Use a peel stripper to peel eight fine strips, ending the grooves shortly before the stem (Figure 2). Place the lily in cold water until it opens up.

RADISH MOUSE

Select a radish with a long root (for the tail) and cut it flat on one side (Figure 3). Place it flat side down. On the top, make two slanted incisions opposite each other and put two pieces of radish into the cuts as ears. Make two holes for the eyes and place a small clove in each (Figure 4).

RADISH SPIRAL

Peel a large white radish and cut off the ends. If you have a spiral radish cutter, use it as shown to make a spiral. If not, simply pierce the radish lengthwise with a wooden or metal skewer. Use a sharp knife to cut all the way around the radish in a spiral fashion, cutting only as far as the skewer. Remove the stick. Gently pull the spiral apart or put it in cold water so it opens up.

CHRYSANTHEMUM

Cut a thick piece of white radish into a ball with a 2-1/2-inch (6 cm) diameter. Cut the top and bottom flat.

Radishes

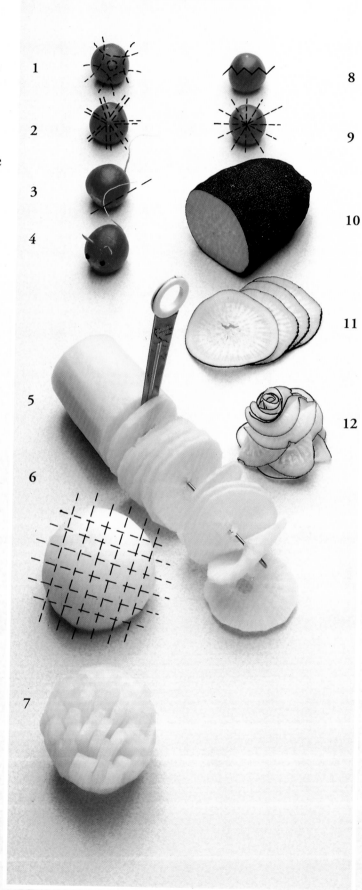

Make checkerboard incisions

from the top almost to the bottom (Figure 6), and place the radish in salted water to soften. Then pull and bend the small petals apart (Figure 7). For a yellow chrysanthemum, add saffron to the water.

RADISH CORONET

Make a zigzag cut around and into the center of the radish (Figure 8). Then twist the top against the bottom to separate the two halves.

RADISH MARGUERITE

Make 12 cuts all around the radish from the top almost to the bottom (Figure 9). Then use a small knife to pull the peel from the flesh down to the stem. Place in cold water until it opens up.

RADISH BLOSSOM

Wash a black radish and cut the root end flat (Figure 10). Shave off thin slices, sprinkle salt on top, and let sit for about five minutes. Rinse and dry off. Arrange the slices in a row, slightly overlapping (Figure 11), and then roll them up, starting from the end with the first slice. Hold the roll on one end and slide a small rubber band over it to hold it together. Cut the slices flat on the tied end to stabilize the blossom. Carefully pull the petals apart and fold them down (Figure 12).

RADISH WITH STAR

Press a star-shaped cookie cutter into a radish and remove it. Then use a knife with a sharp tip to remove the star from the radish.

Mice in Cheese

Radish Coronets
on Zucchini

Radish Rose

Radish Coronet

Radish Rose on Tartlet

Radish Marguerite

Radish With Star

Water Lily

ant Radish Flower

Radish Blossom
on Zucchini

Radish Flower in a Vase

ZUCCHINI BASE
Place a radish coronet on top of a fluted zucchini slice and garnish with cottage cheese or herbs.

MICE IN CHEESE
Place radish mice in a large piece of Swiss cheese.

RADISH FLOWER
Arrange a radish spiral in a ring. Place a radish chrysanthemum in the middle.

ROSE ON TARTLET
Fill a small tartlet with some cottage cheese or herbed cheese spread, and place a radish rose on top.

FLOWER IN A VASE
Place a radish flower in a tall cucumber turret (see page 24). Make two incisions on each side of the turret and insert two cucumber strips for handles. Fasten cutout vegetables to the vase.

Potatoes

POTATO SLICES

Using a smooth or fluted knife, cut a peeled potato into 1/2-inch (1 cm) thick slices (Figure 1). Boil in either salted water, red beet juice, or spinach juice until the slices are tender (Figure 2). For the spinach juice, wash fresh spinach and grind it in a meat grinder. Squeeze the spinach through a piece of cheesecloth and catch the juice in a bowl. Or deep-fry potato slices in hot oil at 350° F (170° C) until they are golden brown (Figure 2).

POTATO MUSHROOMS

Wash and peel a large potato. Use a large melon baller to carve out potato balls (Figure 3). Push an apple corer into the center of the ball and, using a sharp knife, cut away the potato around the corer (Figure 4). Carefully pull out the apple corer. Cook the mushrooms in salted water until tender, refresh under cold water, and drain. For colored mushrooms, boil them in red beet juice or spinach juice.

TRAPPED POTATO

Cut a large, peeled, raw potato into a 1-1/4-inch (3 cm) cube (Figure 5). Carve a square into each side of the cube, about 1/4 inch (1/2 cm) away from the outer edges (Figure 6). Remove the top layer of potato flesh inside the squares. Toward the edges,

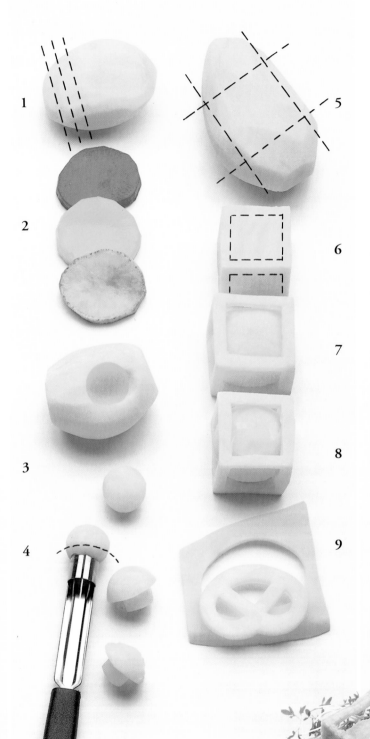

cut deeper into the inner flesh and loosen it from the outer square (Figure 7). The interior flesh will then sit loosely in the square. Finally, cut the interior flesh carefully into a ball shape (Figure 8). Deep-fry the cube in hot oil until it is golden brown.

POTATO PRETZEL

Cut a 1/4-inch (1/2 cm) thick slice of potato. Cut out a pretzel shape with a pretzel cutter and boil in salted water until tender. For colored pretzels, use red beet juice or spinach juice. Another alternative is to deep-fry them at 350° (170° C) until they are golden brown.

POTATO MUSHROOMS IN NEST

Place several potato mushrooms on a nest made from finely grated carrots and zucchini that have been sprinkled with some lemon juice.

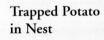

Trapped Potato in Nest

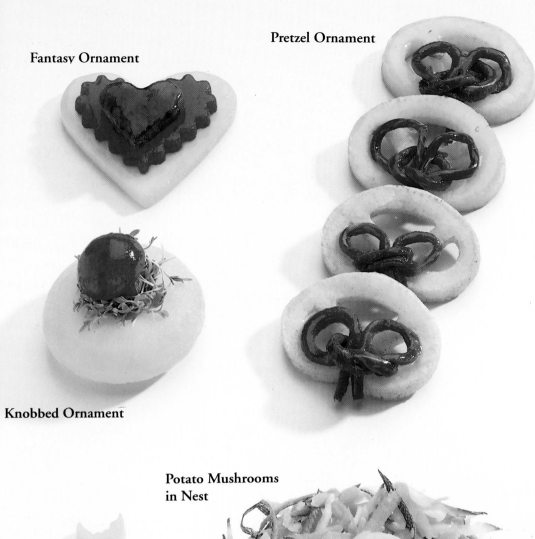

Fantasy Ornament

Pretzel Ornament

Knobbed Ornament

Potato Mushrooms in Nest

Small Aquarium

TRAPPED POTATO IN NEST

Place a trapped, deep-fried potato on a bed of sprouts.

PRETZEL ORNAMENT

Cut out several pretzels, deep-fry them, and arrange them slightly overlapping. Garnish the pretzels with bows made from cured or boiled ham strips.

SMALL AQUARIUM

Blanch some potato slices and cut out small fish shapes. Then boil them in red beet juice or spinach juice and arrange them in a school. Garnish with a sprig of dill.

FANTASY ORNAMENT

Blanch potato slices and cut out different shapes. Boil them in dyed water and arrange ornaments.

KNOBBED ORNAMENT

Blanch a 1/2-inch (1-1/2 cm) thick potato slice and cut out a circle 2-1/2 inches (6 cm) in diameter. Slightly scoop out the middle with a melon baller, boil in water to which you've added a few sprigs of saffron or a few drops of yellow food coloring, and stuff with sprouts. Put a red potato mushroom on top.

MUSHROOM FOR STUFFING

Twist the stem off a large mushroom (Figure 1). Sprinkle some lemon juice on the mushroom head to prevent it from discoloring. Stuff with your favorite filling.

FLUTED MUSHROOM

Cut off the stem level with the head. Then, starting at the top, pull fine strips off the mushroom, using a peel stripper (Figure 2). Sprinkle with lemon juice.

MUSHROOM SLICES

Trim the stem. Cut the mushroom into equal-sized slices (Figure 3) and sprinkle with lemon juice.

Mushrooms

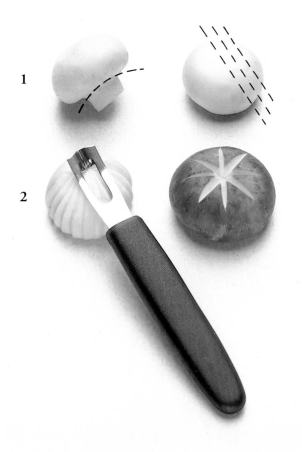

1

2

3

4

CARVED MUSHROOM

Trim the stem of a brown mushroom. Carve out small, wedge-shaped strips at the top, all crossing in the middle to form a star (Figure 4). Sprinkle with lemon juice.

MUSHROOM ON CUCUMBER SLICE

Garnish a fluted, diagonally cut slice of cucumber with tips of asparagus and tomato strips. Top with a fluted mushroom.

STUFFED FLUTED MUSHROOM

Twist the stem out of a fluted mushroom. Using a pastry bag, press liverwurst into the head and garnish it with a small orange segment from which the membranes have been removed (see page 56) and some cutout truffle or cucumber peel.

Stuffed Fluted Mushroom

Mushroom on Cucumber Slice

Stuffed Morels

FOR ABOUT 20 MOREL HALVES:

10 large, dried whole morels

4 teaspoons cooked, frozen spinach

6 teaspoons fine pork sausage stuffing

Salt and pepper

1 cup (250 ml) canned chicken broth

SOAKING TIME:
App. 5 hours

PREPARATION TIME:
App. 25 min.

1. Soak the morels in cold water for about 5 hours. Then carefully rinse and pat dry.

2. Squeeze out the prepared leaf spinach, add salt and pepper to taste, and puree with a hand mixer.

3. Mix the spinach with the sausage. Using a pastry bag with a round tip, press the mixture into the morels.

4. Bring the chicken broth to a boil and cook the stuffed morels in the broth for about 2 minutes. Reduce the heat and let the broth simmer for 5 more minutes. Then allow morels to cool in the broth.

5. Remove the morels, carefully pat dry, and halve them lengthwise. Use them as garnishings, with the cut side up.

FLUTED MUSHROOM ON SQUASH STAR

Cut a piece of yellow squash (using the outside wall and the peel) and cut it into a star shape. Place the fluted mushroom on top of the star and finish off with half a peppercorn.

MUSHROOM SLICE WITH BUTTERFLY

On a large mushroom slice, arrange two cherry tomato wedges for wings. Attach two chive stalks for antennae.

SLICED MUSHROOM ORNAMENT

Arrange mushroom slices in a row, slightly overlapping. Cut different shapes out of red, green, and yellow bell pepper and place them on top of the mushrooms.

Stuffed Morels

Fluted Mushroom on Squash Star

Sliced Mushroom Ornament

Mushroom Slice With Butterfly

37

Stone Fruit

APPLES

These days, apples are grown all over the world. By nature, however, they are the fruit of temperate climates. When they are grown in these areas, the flesh has a firm texture, and the relation of sugar content and acid is well balanced. The earliest seasonal apples are harvested in late summer; later the so-called winter apples ripen. Experiment with the many varieties available, always choosing fresh, seasonal apples. If there are none on the market, fall back on stored fruits. Apples are well suited for garnishings, but don't forget that peeled and cut apples quickly take on a brownish color. To prevent discoloration, drizzle lemon juice on the pieces. An alternative is to poach the apple pieces (see page 40). In addition to fresh apples, small, canned crab apples can also be used for garnishes.

PEARS

Pears are also typical fruits of moderate climates and are available in many different varieties, most of which fall into two categories: the smaller cooking pears, which are usually quite hard and not very juicy, and the eating pears, which have a sweet, juicy flesh. For garnishes only eating pears are suitable. Since pears cannot be stored for very long, they are mostly available in the fall. During the rest of the year it is possible to use canned pears.

Apples

PEELED APPLES

Remove the peel with a peeler, starting at the stem (Figure 1) and spiraling down to the base.

APPLE WEDGES

Use an apple corer to remove the core from a peeled apple (Figure 2), and cut the apple lengthwise in half. Then cut the halves lengthwise into wedges (Figure 3). Or make use of an apple slicer to cut even wedges (Figure 4).

APPLE ROUNDS

For equal-sized slices, use only the middle part of the apple. First cut off a thick slice from the top and bottom of a peeled apple. Then cut the remaining piece crosswise into even slices and use a large, round cutter to cut out circles (Figure 5). Remove the core with a small corer or cutter (Figure 6).

APPLE TURRETS

Cut off a slice from the top and bottom of a peeled apple, leaving the tall center. Use a smooth or ridged cookie cutter to cut out a circle. Press a small, round cutter into the middle (Figure 7). Pull it out and scoop out the center with a melon baller (Figure 8).

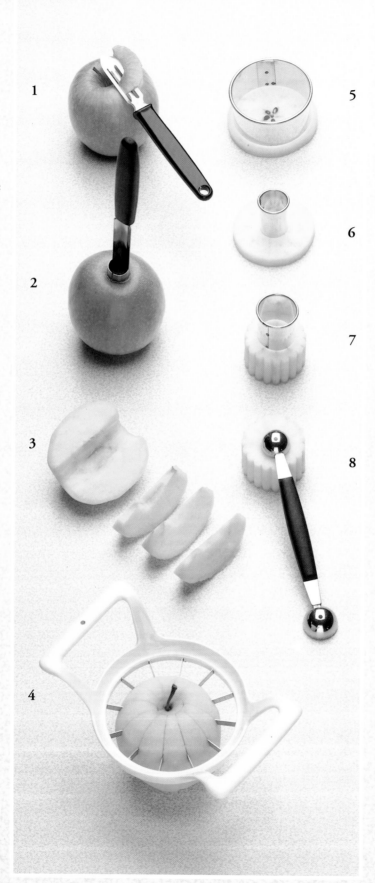

1

2

3

4

5

6

7

8

POACHED APPLES

When prepared in advance, apples tend to discolor. For garnishings, therefore, either sprinkle them with lemon juice or poach them. When poaching, shape the apples the desired way first and then cook them over low heat in white wine until slightly undercooked. For better taste, add lemon juice, sugar, and a small cinnamon stick to the white wine. Allow the poached pieces to cool off in the liquid, then drain and pat dry.

BAKED APPLE SLICES

To pan-fry, dredge the poached, dried-off apple slices in flour and fry them in butter until golden brown. To deep-fry them, blend an egg with some flour and dip the slices in the batter. Then coat them with grated coconut, almond slices, or almond slivers. Deep-fry at 360° F (180° C) until golden brown.

APPLE TURRET WITH AMARETTO CREAM AND GRAPE

Make a small cut at the top of a red grape and push an almond into the cut. Place the grape on top of the cream-filled turret and insert some toasted almond slices into the Amaretto cream.

FOR 10 APPLE TURRETS:

2 teaspoons unflavored
  gelatin
2 ounces (60 g) Amaretti
  (Italian almond cookies)
1 cup (250 g) ricotta
  cheese
1 tablespoon Amaretto
10 apple towers

PREPARATION TIME:
App. 20 min.

1. Soak the gelatin in 3 tablespoons cold water. Then heat the mixture, stirring constantly until all granules are dissolved.

2. In a blender or food processor, process the Amaretti until they are fine crumbs. Again using a blender or processor, whip the ricotta until it is very smooth. Stir the Amaretti crumbs and Amaretto into the ricotta, then stir in the dissolved gelatin. Refrigerate.

3. Shortly before the cream starts to gel, press it into the apple towers, using a pastry bag with a star-shaped tip.

APPLE TURRET WITH MELON BALL

Combine 1 cup (250 ml) white wine, 2 tablespoons sugar, 1/4 cinnamon stick, some grated lemon peel, and a few threads of saffron. Bring to a simmer, add an apple turret, and let simmer for about 4 minutes. Then drain the liquid off. Place a cantaloupe ball (see page 54) on top. Garnish with raisins, nuts, or cutout pieces of black olive.

BAKED APPLE SLICE WITH LITCHI

Deep-fry an apple slice coated with grated coconut and place a peeled litchi on top. Garnish it with a green cocktail cherry. Around it place small wedges of candied cherries.

BAKED APPLE SLICE WITH PLUM

Deep-fry an apple slice coated with sliced almonds and place a soft plum on top. Insert a peeled, whole almond in the middle. Garnish the apple slice with pistachio nuts; thin, cooked strips of orange peel; and orange segments.

**Apple Turret
With Melon Ball**

**Apple Turrets
With Amaretto Cream
and Grape**

**Baked Apple Slice
With Litchi**

Apples

APPLE SWAN

Use a quarter of an unpeeled, red apple. (Leave the core in the apple.) Working from the peel side, remove a V-shaped piece of apple, cutting about 1/8 inch (3 mm) from the edges (Figure 1). From the smaller piece, remove another V-shaped piece (Figure 2). Continue cutting out V-shaped pieces all the way to the middle. Sprinkle some lemon juice on the cut surfaces. Put the apple quarter back together, slightly staggered (Figure 3). Cut a swan neck out of an apple piece and place it on the body.

APPLE BOATS

Halve an unpeeled, red apple. (Leave the core in the apple.) Place the apple half cut side down. Using a sharp knife, cut a short, narrow, V-shaped piece out of the middle (Figure 4) and set it aside. Follow the lines of the first wedge and cut out another, larger V-shaped piece. Repeat this process two more times (Figure 5), and cut the four removed wedges in half across the middle. Sprinkle lemon juice on the cut surfaces. Put the cut wedges back into the large apple piece and move them slightly to the side to produce a layered effect (Figure 6).

APPLE WINGS

Use a quarter of an unpeeled, red apple. (Leave the core in the apple.) Using a sharp knife with a pointed tip, cut a triangular piece out of one of the ends (Figure 7). Sprinkle lemon juice on the cut surface. Cut out two equal-sized V-shaped pieces (Figure 8) and fill the holes with green gelatin (mint or lime).

APPLE SWAN WITH LAKE

The swan floats in a lake of blue aspic. To make the aspic, sprinkle 1 envelope of unflavored gelatin over 1/4 cup (60 ml) of white wine to soften. Place the wine-gelatin mixture in a saucepan with another 1/4 cup of white wine and 1/2 cup (120 ml) blue Curacao. Simmer, stirring constantly, until the granules are completely dissolved. Add 2 tablespoons of sugar and a squirt of lemon juice, pour the mixture into a flat bowl, and allow it to gel. Use a knife to cut out a "lake" shape, and place an apple swan on top of it.

Apple Swan With Lake

Colorful Apple Boat

Apple Swan on Pear

Apple Wings

Orange Slice With Miniature Apple

Apple Butterfly

COLORFUL APPLE BOAT

Use one red and one green apple half (both should be the same size) and prepare apple boats of both. Then put the pieces together alternating the colors, and make two multi-colored boats.

APPLE BUTTERFLY

Using a pastry bag with a round tip, press Amaretto Cream (see page 41) on top of a long, thin cookie. For wings, use four V-shaped apple segments (see directions for the Apple Swan) and place two thin pieces of vanilla bean into the cream for antennae. For the eyes, press two small pieces of a red cocktail cherry into the cream.

APPLE SWAN ON PEAR

Poach a pear quarter and pipe a large rosette of Amaretto Cream (see page 41) on top, using a pastry bag with a star-shaped tip. Place the apple swan on the cream.

ORANGE SLICE WITH MINIATURE APPLE

Place a miniature apple in the middle of a peeled orange slice. All around it, pipe rosettes of Amaretto Cream (see page 41) and garnish with red currants.

43

Pears

PEELING PEARS
Peel the pear lengthwise from the stem to the base with a peeler (Figure 1).

PEAR HALVES
Cut a peeled pear lengthwise in half. Remove the seeds with a melon baller (Figure 2). Cut out the stem and the base.

PEAR FAN
Peel, halve, and core a pear. Combine 1 cup (250 ml) water, 1 cup white wine, and 1/2 cup (125 g) sugar to a boil. Reduce to a simmer, add the pear to the syrup, and cook briefly. Allow the pear to cool in the syrup. Use a small knife to make comblike cuts into the pear, from the base almost to the stem (Figure 3). Then press carefully on the pear so that the fan unfolds.

POACHED PEARS
Since pears discolor when prepared too far in advance, either sprinkle them with lemon juice or poach them. For poaching, bring a mixture of white wine, some lemon juice, sugar, a cinnamon stick, and a clove to a boil, and simmer the pear halves in the mixture until tender. Allow the pears to cool in the syrup and then drain.

ORNAMENTAL PEAR WEDGES
Cut an unpeeled pear half into wedges. Use a knife to remove a V-shaped piece from the peel side of every wedge. Arrange the wedges and top with a cape gooseberry or other exotic fruit.

PEAR FAN WITH MINT
Garnish a pear fan with unblemished mint leaves.

1

2

3

Pear-Kiwi Windmill

Pear Hedgehog

44

Pear Halves With Cheese Cream

FOR 8 PEAR HALVES:
1-1/2 cups (250 g) wild
    berries (fresh or frozen)
3 eggs
1/2 cup (100 g) sugar
1 cup (200 g) cream
    cheese, Neufchatel,
    or ricotta
8 poached pear halves

PREPARATION TIME:
App. 15 min.

1. Clean and wash the fresh berries or thaw frozen berries; drain.

2. Separate the eggs. Beat egg yolks with sugar until creamy. Wash the beaters carefully, then beat the egg whites until stiff.

3. Stir the cheese into the egg-sugar mixture and carefully blend in the egg whites.

4. To serve, press the egg-cheese into the pear halves and garnish with berries.

PEAR-KIWI WINDMILL

Using a ridged, round cookie cutter, cut a circle out of a thick, peeled pear slice and poach it. Cut a kiwi into six wedges. Remove a wedge-shaped piece from the wider side of the kiwi wedges to create V-shaped kiwi pieces (see Apple Swan, page 42). Place them on the pear base, together with a cherry.

PEAR LANTERN

Make a zigzag cut around and into the center of the upper half of a pear. Twist the two parts against each other to separate the halves. Peel the bottom half and cut the base flat. Carefully scoop it out and poach it. Stuff it with Waldorf salad (see the recipe on page 58, but substitute pears for apples) and place the upper half back on top.

PEAR HEDGEHOG

Place a poached pear half cut side down, and spike it with toasted almond slivers. For the eyes, cut two small holes and push raisins into them.

PEAR TURRET WITH CRAB APPLE

Garnish a pear turret with a crab apple and orange slices.

Pear Lantern

Pear Halves With Cheese Cream

Pear Turret With Crab Apple

Ornamental Pear Wedges

Pear Fan With Mint

Tropical and Citrus Fruit

BANANAS

The disadvantage of garnishing with bananas is that they turn brown rapidly. To slow discoloration, drizzle lemon juice on the exposed surfaces. For garnishes, use barely ripe bananas with firm, light yellow flesh. For eating, allow them to ripen further. If they are not ripe at the time of purchase, store them at room temperature. Never store them in the refrigerator; the cold will interrupt their ripening process and turn them slightly bitter.

CARAMBOLE (STAR FRUIT)

Often called star fruit because of their intriguing shape, caramboles are very popular for garnishes. Slices are typically used, since they resemble stars. The fruit is truly ripe when the flesh has turned amber-colored. Then its taste is slightly sour and reminiscent of a gooseberry or quince. Star fruit can be stored for only a short time in the refrigerator. The lengthwise edges soon turn brown.

KIWIS

This egg-sized fruit is also called a Chinese gooseberry. Today, it comes to the stores throughout the year from New Zealand. Kiwis are ripe when they give slightly to pressure and when the flesh is bright green. The sour, aromatic taste is reminiscent of the gooseberry. Kiwis can be stored for about two weeks in the vegetable drawer of the refrigerator.

LEMONS

Available throughout the year, lemons are invaluable for their vibrant color and sharp scent. The use of untreated fruit is recommended, especially when the peel is used.

LIMES

In well-stocked grocery stores, limes are available throughout the year. The lime's peel is thinner than lemon peel, and its greenish flesh is more intense in taste. Unlike lemons and oranges, limes are usually untreated. Because of their thin peel, they cannot be stored for long before they shrivel up. Store them in the refrigerator.

MELONS

These days a number of varieties are available. Watermelons add splendid color but little aroma. Other melons add both. Best known is the cantaloupe, with its yellow-green peel and sweet, orange flesh. The honeydew is also popular: its yellow-green peel and aromatic, greenish-white flesh add an elegant touch. Less common varieties are well worth investigating. Rinds range from brilliant yellow to green-and-gold-striped, and the flesh can be honey yellow or shocking apricot. You can't determine ripeness by the look of the rind. Rather, try scent and touch. The stem end should have a sweet, fruity aroma, and the opposite end should give slightly to pressure. Store melons in the vegetable compartment of the refrigerator or in a cool room.

ORANGES

Oranges with light-colored peel and orange-colored flesh are available throughout the year. Between December and March, specialty markets may carry blood oranges, whose flesh is blood red. The many varieties of oranges differ in taste, juiciness, and peel thickness. The same variety may vary markedly in all those characteristics, depending upon where it was grown. If you are using the peel for garnishings, untreated fruit is best.

PINEAPPLES

Available throughout the year, this tropical fruit is sweet-sour and aromatic. It is usually ripe when the color of the peel ranges from dark orange to copper, the fruit has a sweet scent, and the end opposite the stem yields slightly to pressure. Pineapples cannot take cold temperature. Store them in a cool room, rather than in the refrigerator, and try to avoid bruising them. If fresh pineapples are not available for garnishing, canned pineapple slices are an alternative. However, these are much sweeter than the fresh fruit.

Pineapples

PINEAPPLE BOWL

Cut a large slice length-wise off a pineapple (Figure 1). Leave the stem as is or halve it. Cut around the flesh 3/4 inch (2 cm) from the edge, and remove the flesh with a grape-fruit knife or a large tablespoon (Figure 2). Fill the pineapple bowl as desired.

PEELING A PINEAPPLE

Cut the stem and the base off the pineapple, using a large knife. Then remove the brown peel in small, 1/2-inch (1 cm) thick strips with a sharp knife (Figure 3). Cut out the brown eyes, making wedge-shaped cuts following the lines of the eyes (Figure 4).

PINEAPPLE SLICES

Cut a peeled pineapple crosswise into slices about 1-1/2 inches (2 cm) thick, using a large knife. With a small, round cookie cutter, cut out the hard core (Figure 5). It is also possible to make slices from an unpeeled pineapple. Cut off the stem and the base and cut the pineapple into slices about 1-1/2 inches (2 cm) thick. Remove the peel with a large, round cookie or biscuit cutter (Figure 6) and the hard core with a small, round cutter.

COOKED PINEAPPLE SLICES

Dip pineapple slices in flour and then in beaten egg. Coat them with grated coconut or almond slices and deep-fry at 350° F (180° C) until the batter is golden.

PINEAPPLE TROPICAL ISLAND

The island is pictured on page 50. Choose a pineapple with an attractive stem. Cut the base flat and peel the pineapple. Leave some peel at the bottom for the "tree root" (Figure 7). Then remove the flesh with a knife all the way to the hard core (Figure 8). Again, leave some flesh for the root. Cut the flesh into cubes and set aside. Make a second palm tree in the same manner. Pin some red grapes to the leaves and the upper end of the hard core, using pins or small wooden toothpicks. Place the palm trees on a flat plate and arrange the flesh around them. If desired, sprinkle with cherry liqueur.

Pineapple Ornaments

Baked Pineapple Slice With Fruit

Pineapple Flower

Pineapple Butterfly

PINEAPPLE BUTTERFLY

Cut pineapple slices into quarters. Cut a small wedge out of the outer edge of two quarters. Place the pieces to the right and the left of a strawberry half and garnish with slices of red cocktail cherries and peppercorns. Place two thin pieces of vanilla bean at the top of the strawberry for antennae.

PINEAPPLE FLOWER

From a peeled pineapple, cut a thin, 3/4-inch (2 cm) wide spiral strip of flesh. Then roll up the spiral and place it in the hole of a pineapple slice. Garnish the slice with angelica or mint leaves and strawberry quarters.

PINEAPPLE ORNAMENTS

Arrange four quarters of a pineapple slice in a row. Garnish each quarter with a strawberry quarter, a pistachio nut, two red peppercorns, and a mint leaf.

BAKED PINEAPPLE SLICE WITH FRUIT

Coat a pineapple slice with grated coconut and bake it. Place a red cocktail cherry with stem in the middle. Make lengthwise cuts into red and green grapes, arrange them around the cherry, and insert small tangerine segments in the cuts.

Pineapple Bowl With Exotic Fruit Salad

FOR 1 PINEAPPLE BOWL:
1 tamarillo (tree tomato)
1 miniature pineapple
1 kiwi
1 papaya
8 litchis
1 carambole (star fruit)
1 mango
1/8 teaspoon cayenne
    pepper
1/8 teaspoon cardamon
Dash Pernod
1/4 cup (60 ml) sugar
    syrup
Dash rose water
Juice of one lime
1 pineapple bowl
Lemon balm or mint
    leaves

PREPARATION TIME:
App. 20 min.

1. Peel the tamarillo, the miniature pineapple, and the kiwi. Peel the papaya, halve it, and scoop out the seeds. Peel the litchis and remove the seeds. Cut all of the fruit, including the star fruit, into evenly thick slices. Carve small balls out of the papaya.

2. Season the fruit pieces with cayenne pepper and cardamon. Combine the Pernod, sugar syrup, rose water, and lime juice, and pour over the fruit.

3. Peel the mango. Remove the flesh from the seed, cube it, and puree it in the blender. Stir the puree into the fruit.

4. To serve, spoon the fruit into the pineapple bowls or place it in layers, one type at a time. Garnish with the herb leaves.

**Pineapple Bowl
With Exotic Fruit**

Pineapple Islands

50

1 small package green
    gelatin dessert (lime,
    mint, etc.)
1 teaspoon unflavored
    gelatin
3 tablespoons Mascarpone
Grated orange peel from
    1/2 orange
1 egg yolk
1 tablespoon sugar
1/2 cup (40 g) whipped
    cream
1 small package straw-
    berry gelatin

Bananas
Colorful Banana Slices

The striped effect is produced by pouring three liquid layers, one at a time, into an empty banana peel, allowing each layer to gel before adding another, and slicing the banana crosswise.

1. Cut a small strip out of the inner side of the peel of each banana (keep the strips). Carefully scoop out the banana with a melon baller. The flesh will not be used.

2. Prepare the green gelatin according to package instructions. Let it cool slightly and pour it, still liquid, into banana peels until each peel is about 1/3 full. Chill for 1 hour.

3. To prepare the Mascarpone cream, sprinkle the unflavored gelatin over 2 tablespoons cold water and allow to soften for about 10 minutes. Meanwhile, push the Mascarpone through a fine sieve and mix with the orange peel, the egg yolk, and the sugar.

4. Heat the gelatin mixture and simmer it, stirring constantly, until all the granules are dissolved. Let it cool slightly, then add it to the Mascarpone cream. Mix in the whipped cream, spoon the mixture into the bananas, and allow to harden in the refrigerator for about 1 hour.

5. Prepare the strawberry gelatin according to package instructions. Let the mixture cool slightly and pour the still-liquid gelatin into the bananas. Close off the banana peel with the strip set aside and allow all of it to harden in the refrigerator for 1 hour.

6. When the strawberry gelatin is firm, cut the bananas crosswise into slices.

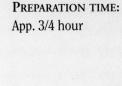

51

Carambole (Star Fruit) and Kiwi

CARAMBOLE SLICES AND BASES

Use a knife to cut a washed star fruit crosswise into 1/2-inch (1 cm) thick slices (Figure 1). Sprinkle lemon juice on them to prevent discoloring. The two end pieces (Figure 2) can be used as bases.

KIWI CORONET

Make a zigzag cut around and into the center of the kiwi, then twist the halves against each other and separate them (Figure 3). Cut the bottoms of the coronets flat.

PEELING A KIWI

Peel a kiwi from top to bottom in one spiral piece with a peeler (Figure 4).

KIWI SLICES

Cut a peeled kiwi into 1/4- to 1/2-inch (1/2 to 1 cm) thick slices. The slices can be cut crosswise (Figure 5) or lengthwise (Figure 6) from top to bottom.

CARAMBOLE STAR

Put a few kernels of canned corn in a large melon baller and add liquid aspic. (See the recipe on page 42, but use all wine for the liquid.) Let the aspic harden in the refrigerator for 1 hour. Dip the melon baller halfway into hot water and remove the corn aspic. Place two star fruit slices staggered on top of each other. Cut small triangles out of peeled red and green bell pepper pieces, and place them on the tips of the star fruit corners. Place the aspic half-ball in the middle.

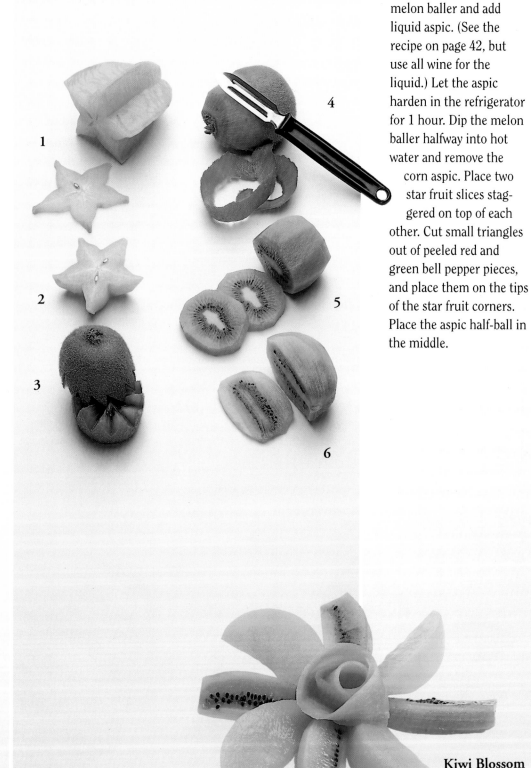

Carambole Candle

Kiwi Blossom

CARAMBOLE SLICES WITH KIWI CORONET

Place a kiwi coronet on top of a star fruit slice. Form a ball out of 1/2 teaspoon cream cheese, using your hands. Roll the ball in sweet paprika powder and place it on top of the kiwi coronet.

ORNAMENT FROM CARAMBOLE SLICES

Place four star fruit slices in a row, slightly overlapping each other. Make a cut halfway down the middle of two fresh litchis so that the pit is visible. Pull down the fine cover on some cape gooseberries. Place litchis and gooseberries on top of the star fruit slices.

Ornament From Carambole Slices

Carambole Star

CARAMBOLE CANDLE

Place a long piece of heart of palm on top of a star fruit slice. Insert half a red pepper in the top.

ORNAMENT FROM KIWI SLICES

Cut peeled kiwi into slices. Then cut small, round slices of mango or other colorful fruit into circles and lay them on the kiwi. Top with halved grapes and arrange them in a row, slightly overlapping. Then cut out oval kiwi slices and also top them with mango and grapes. Arrange them in the same way next to the first fruit row.

KIWI BLOSSOM

Cut a peeled kiwi lengthwise into wedges. Do the same with a peeled peach. Arrange the wedges, alternating kiwi and peach, into a blossom. Use a peeler to cut a thin, 1/2-inch (1 cm) wide strip of flesh from a peeled papaya. Roll the strip into a small rose and place it in the middle of the blossom.

Carambole Slice With Cape Gooseberry

Ornament From Kiwi Slices

Carambole Slices With Kiwi Coronet

53

FILLED MELON

Use a large knife to cut a melon in half crosswise. Remove the seeds and pulp, scraping the flesh with a spoon (Figure 1). Cut the bottoms flat to make them stable, and fill to your liking.

MELON CORONET

Using a pointed knife, make a zigzag cut all the way around and into the center of the melon. Twist the halves in opposite directions to separate them. Remove the seeds with a spoon, cut the bottoms flat, and fill to your liking.

MELON BASKET

Cut lengthwise about 1/3 into the melon, positioning the cut slightly off center (see Figure 3). Make a similar cut on the other side, leaving a piece in the middle for the handle. Cut down vertically to meet the end of each cut, thus forming a handle. Remove the melon wedges. Cut over the horizontal cuts in a zigzag pattern. Cut the flesh off the handle, leaving about 1/4 to 1/2 inch (1/2 to 1 cm). Remove the seeds and pulp with a spoon, and cut the bottom flat. Fill the basket to your liking.

Melons

MELON WEDGES

Cut a melon lengthwise into six or eight wedges. Remove the seeds with a spoon (Figure 4). To serve wedges, use a curved grapefruit knife to cut the peel off the flesh (Figure 5). Leave the wedge sitting on the peel and cut it into bite-size pieces, using a smooth or fluted knife (Figure 6).

MELON BALLS

Remove the seeds from a melon and press a melon baller firmly into the flesh. With a twist, scoop out small balls (Figure 7).

FILLED MELON BASKET

Combine 1 cup (150 g) canned pickled fruit, a few melon balls, and 1/8 cup (30 ml) port wine, and place in the melon basket. To garnish the handle, cut small, red grapes in half, lay each one on a kumquat slice, and attach them to the handle, using small pieces of wooden toothpicks.

Stuffed Melon Basket

Melon Star

Melon Grape Cluster

Colorful Melon Slices

MELON STAR

Cut a small lid off a melon using the same technique as for a melon coronet. Then cut the peel side flat so the melon sits firmly. Place a tomato rose (see page 12) in the middle and garnish with mint leaves. Place tiny watermelon balls or cocktail cherries between the ridges.

MELON GRAPE CLUSTER

Arrange a grape cluster from melon balls and attach a stem using candied angelica.

COLORFUL MELON SLICES

Cut a melon in half and remove the pulp and seeds. Add layers of gelatin in different colors, using the technique described for Colorful Banana Slices, page 51, so that the layers don't blend into each other. When all the fillings have hardened, cut the melon into 1/2-inch (1-1/2 cm) thick slices. Then garnish the slices with small fruit pieces (grapes, gooseberries, and others).

55

FLUTED CITRUS

Using a peel stripper, cut thin strips of peel off the fruit (Figure 1). Then cut the fluted fruit into thin slices (Figure 2).

LEMON AND ORANGE BASKETS

Cut out two wedges from the top of a lemon or an orange, then cut the bottom of the basket level (Figure 3). Use a spoon to remove the flesh from the handle and the basket, then fill.

ROTARY LEMON

Cut 1/3 off the top of a lemon and cut the bottom flat (Figure 4). Discard the smaller piece. On the large piece, make five vertical cuts into the top surface at equal distances (Figure 5). Starting with any cut, make a cut diagonally down toward the end of the next cut (Figure 6). Repeat four more times and remove the pieces.

Lemons and Oranges

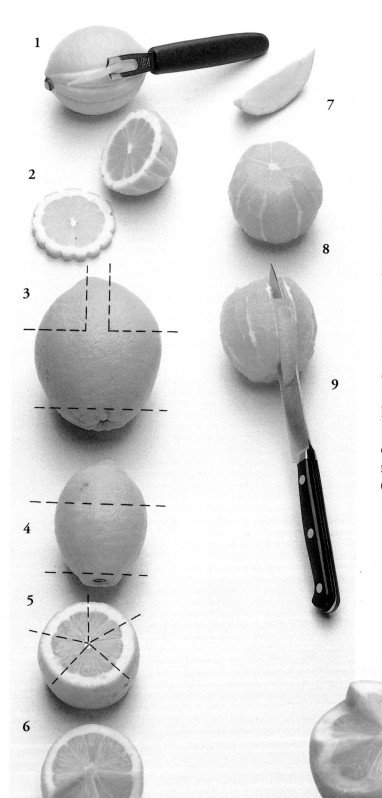

1
2
3
4
5
6
7
8
9

Rotary Lemon

WEDGES WITH PEEL

Cut oranges or lemons lengthwise in half with a knife and then cut wedges (Figure 7).

ORANGE SEGMENTS

Carefully peel an orange and remove the white pith completely (Figure 8). Using a sharp knife, cut into the orange close to the membrane all the way to the center. Lift out the segments (Figure 9).

LEMON BASKET WITH CRANBERRY HORSERADISH CREAM

For the filling, mix 1/2 teaspoon canned cranberry sauce with 1/8 teaspoon prepared horseradish. Blend in 1/2 tablespoon whipping cream and spoon the mixture into the basket. Garnish with cranberries.

56

Filled Orange Basket

Orange Slice With Gold Foil

Lemon Basket With Cranberry Horseradish Cream

Lemon Spiral

Orange Slice With Soft Plum

ORANGE SLICE WITH SOFT PLUM

Place a soft plum on top of a carefully peeled orange slice and lay red currants around the plum.

LEMON SPIRAL

Use a peel stripper to cut a peel spiral. Make sure it does not break. Leave the spiral attached to the lemon and arrange it next to the fruit in a decorative way.

FILLED ORANGE BASKET

Use an orange with a thick peel. From the top of the orange to the lower third, pull fine peel strips down the orange, using a peel stripper and leaving the strip attached to the fruit. Then cut the orange into a basket and scoop out the flesh. Form the citrus peel strips into curls and tie a peel strip to the handle. Fill the basket with fruit cocktail.

ORANGE SLICE WITH GOLD FOIL

Place a soft plum on a carefully peeled orange slice and cover with gold foil.

Orange Basket With Waldorf Salad

FOR 8 BASKETS:

2 cups (250 g) tart apples
2 cups (250 g) celery bulb
2 cups (250 g) canned
  pineapple pieces
Juice from 1/2 lemon
1/3 cup (100 g)
  mayonnaise
4 teaspoons cream
Salt
White pepper
Sugar
8 orange baskets
3/4 cup (100 g) chopped
  walnuts

PREPARATION TIME:
App. 15 min.

1. Peel the apple, cut in quarters, remove the core, and cut in thin strips. Peel the celery, wash, and also cut into thin strips. Mix both with the drained pineapple pieces and the lemon juice.

2. Blend the mayonnaise with the cream and add salt, pepper, and sugar to taste. Mix the dressing with the salad.

3. Spoon the salad into the orange baskets and garnish with chopped walnuts.

**Orange Basket
With Waldorf Salad**

Lemon Sailboat

Lime Wedge

LEMON SAILBOAT
Insert a wooden pick through both ends of a cornichon slice (or other small pickle) so it forms a sail. Place a lemon wedge on top of a lime slice and insert the pick into both fruit pieces. Stick a caper on the top end of the wooden pick.

ORANGE FLOWER
Using orange and lime segments, a strip of angelica (or other green stem), and pistachio nut halves, arrange a flower with stem and leaves. Garnish the flower petals with chocolate chips.

LIME WEDGE
Cut two rhomboid shapes out of angelica and place the shapes next to a lime wedge or a lime segment.

Orange Flower

Salmon Roses

Orange Segments With Cherry

Lime Segment

ORANGE SEGMENTS WITH CHERRY
Garnish three orange segments with a cocktail cherry with stem.

SALMON ROSES
Roll up two thin smoked salmon slices into rosettes and place them at the ends of a forked parsley sprig. Arrange two lime segments at the stem.

Herbs and Flowers

Fresh herbs and flowers are the ultimate garnishes. They add beauty, fragrance, and a sense of freshness to just about any type of food.

When shopping for fresh herbs, look for strong fragrance, good coloration, and healthy stems. When fresh herbs are shaken, the leaves should stay firmly attached to their stems.

Treat long-stemmed herbs like cut flowers, immersing them in a vase of water and refrigerating them. For protection, cover them loosely with a plastic bag.

Edible flowers can be utilized in a variety of ways. Sprinkle petals on top of cheeses and desserts. Use whole large blossoms to garnish roasts, hors d'oeuvres platters, and soup tureens.

Note that some flowers are toxic. Before garnishing with a new variety, be certain to check a reliable source to make sure the flowers really are edible.

HERB BUNDLES

A wonderfully simple garnishing technique is to tie up
bundles of fresh herbs with raffia, ribbon, or decorative cord.
One option is to select herbs that are used in the dish itself.
You can also choose herbs whose fragrance complements the
food being served or whose colors and shapes work particu-
larly well with the food or the table setting. The examples
below include rosemary skewers tied with raffia, purple basil
tied with magenta ribbon, green basil tied with beige ribbon,
and cilantro wrapped with decorative cord.

POTATO CHIPS WITH HERB SILHOUETTES

For these homemade potato chips, the herb garnishes are intriguingly silhouetted on the food itself. To make the chips, peel and thinly slice the desired amount of good-quality, waxy-type potatoes. Grease a baking sheet with oil or melted butter, and arrange a single layer of potato slices on it. Lay an herb sprig on each one and top with a second slice of potato, pressing down to flatten the herb. Cover with well-buttered parchment paper or baking paper, weigh everything down with another baking sheet, and bake at 400° F (200° C) for 10 to 15 minutes. Remove the potato chips to paper towels to drain and cool.

HERBED TOAST POINTS

Buttered toast doesn't have much pizzazz— unless you garnish it with fresh herbs. Thinly slice a mixture of white and whole-grain breads. Trim the crusts and cut the bread diagonally in half. Arrange the slices on a baking sheet in a single layer, and sprinkle assorted herbs on top. Brush with melted butter and bake at 350° F (125° C) until golden brown.

CHEESE TRAY

The clean, sharp fragrance of herbs provides a perfect counterpoint to rich foods such as cheese and fatty meats. Especially pungent, sage leaves make an excellent addition to a cheese tray garnished with fresh herbs and flowers. To create a decorative tray, arrange a variety of cheeses in an attractive container—a flat basket, for example. Fill the remaining spaces with sprigs of various herbs and a few fresh flowers.

67

Soups

Universally loved, soups are fun to garnish. At left, fresh basil leaves encircle a bowl of tomato soup. In the center, a clear consomme allows the decorations in the bottom of the bowl to show through: sliced scallops, julienne vegetables, and saffron. To garnish onion soup, sprinkle chives, bacon bits, and croutons across the top.

CREOLE TOMATO SOUP

1 green bell pepper
1 small yellow onion
1 tablespoon chopped garlic
1/2 cup (50 g) chopped carrot
1 tablespoon olive oil
1 16-ounce (453 g) can tomatoes
2 cups (500 ml) chicken stock
  or tomato juice

1/4 cup (1/2 g) chopped cilantro
1/4 teaspoon cumin
1 teaspoon gumbo filé powder
1 tablespoon Tabasco or other
  red pepper sauce
1 tablespoon salt
1/4 teaspoon cayenne
2 bay leaves

Medium dice the bell pepper and onion. Place in a soup pot with the garlic, carrots, and olive oil, and saute for 15 minutes. Chop the tomatoes and add them to the pot, along with the chicken stock or tomato juice. Add the remaining ingredients and simmer for 1 hour. The soup may be pureed or served as is. Remove bay leaves before pureeing or serving.

SEAFOOD SAFFRON CONSOMME

1 pound mixed seafood
1 small bunch each fresh parsley, tarragon,
  and thyme
1 small onion
1 carrot
1 stalk celery
1 small leek
6 egg whites
2 cups (500 ml) sherry or sake
1 good pinch saffron
1 tablespoon salt
1/2 teaspoon white pepper
1 gallon (4-1/2 l) fish stock

SWEET ONION SOUP WITH BACON AND CHIVES

6 slices bacon, diced
1 medium sweet onion, peeled and sliced
2 tablespoons flour
1 (1 l) quart chicken stock
1 cup (250 ml) sherry
Salt and pepper
1 cup (250 ml) half and half
1/4 cup (1/2 g) chopped chives

In a heavy soup pot, cook the bacon on low heat until well browned. Add the onions and cook until translucent. Stir in the flour and slowly add the chicken stock. Add the sherry and season to taste with salt and pepper. Bring to a boil while stirring occasionally. Add the cream and the chives and simmer on low heat for 30 minutes.

Finely chop or grind seafood, herbs, and vegetables, and place in a large mixing bowl. Add egg whites, sherry, saffron, salt, and pepper. Bring the fish stock to lukewarm in a saucepan and stir in the other ingredients. Bring the mixture to a simmer, stirring for 10 minutes to prevent scorching. Gradually the vegetable-fish-egg mixture will start to coagulate and float to the top of the stock, forming a "raft." Do NOT stir once the raft begins to form. Simmer 45 minutes, remove from the heat, and let stand 20 minutes. Remove as much of the raft as possible without breaking it up. Strain the consomme through cheesecloth. Arrange garnishes on the bottom of each serving bowl and carefully spoon in the consomme.

HERBAL WREATH

A wreath composed of fresh herbs and other common garnishes is a stunning centerpiece for table or buffet. To make one, cut out a wreath-shaped backing of cardboard. Then add your raw materials, working from bottom layer to top layer all the way around the wreath. First, arrange large leaves around the circumference, to serve as a background; firm, green lettuce works well. Then select sprigs of fresh, colorful herbs—sage and purple basil, for example—and arrange them evenly around the wreath. (If necessary, the herbs can be attached with U-shaped pins; but, left to themselves, they will probably stay more or less where you put them.) Then insert the flimsier foliage—sprigs of fresh thyme and other small-leaved herbs—and group the other garnishes on top: green and red olives; small, colorful peppers; cornichons or other small pickles; and anything else that strikes your fancy.

Leeks and Onions

LEEK PACKAGES AND BUNDLES

To make the square leek packages shown at left, select unblemished leaves from a leek and wash them thoroughly. Blanch them briefly in boiling water, then plunge them into ice water, to make them pliable. For each package, cut a rectangle about 3 inches (7 cm) long and 2 inches (5 cm) wide, and also cut two long, narrow strips for the ties. Using a thin, sharp knife, separate each rectangle into two thin layers. (The layers are fairly well defined and not difficult to separate.) Starting at each corner, cut diagonally toward the center about 1/2 inch (1 cm), to make folding easier. Select a filling that will hold its shape—sushi or flavored rice, for example—and shape a small amount into a square. (A small spatula is helpful for producing flat sides.) Place the filling in the center and fold up the four sides. The thin, moist leek will adhere to itself long enough for you to tie it up with the two thin strips. To make the round bundle at the bottom right of the plate, place a rounded dollop of filling on the rectangle, gather up the sides, and tie it with a long strip.

RED ONION CHRYSANTHEMUM

Select a firm, red onion with no soft spots. Cut off the sprout end only, leaving the root end intact, and peel the onion. Using a thin, sharp knife, cut down into the onion almost to the root. Make another cut at a 90° angle to the first. Continue making cuts, bisecting each angle formed until you can cut no further. Place the onion in cold water and refrigerate overnight. If additional color is desired, add a few drops of food coloring to the water before refrigerating.

SCALLION FLOWERS

Scallion flowers can be made in a variety of ways. To curl the white, or root, end, trim the roots off where they join the onion, and cut the green tip off 2 inches (5 cm) above the white part. Peel away any wilted outer layers. Cut straight through the onion at the root end, then make another cut at a 90° angle to the previous one. Continue for at least two more cuts. Place the scallion in cold water and refrigerate overnight. To curl the green end, cut straight down into the stem of the scallion, again making 90° cuts, and refrigerate in water overnight.

BRIE WITH JOHNNY JUMP-UPS

Select an unblemished round of brie. Arrange a fan-shaped bouquet, using chives for the stems, johnny jump-ups for the flowers, and small sprigs of herbs for extra foliage.

Cookie Bouquet

Flowers and foliage do not have to be limited to a centerpiece for the table. They can also be placed in the center of the food itself. Make meringue cookies, using the recipe from your favorite cookbook and piping the batter from a pastry bag. Dip the cooled cookies in melted semisweet chocolate. Place a small vase of seasonal flowers in the center of a serving plate, and arrange the cookies around the outside.

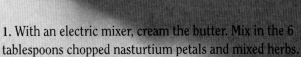

Nasturtium Compound Butter

Nasturtiums are native to South America. Their peppery, sharp-flavored petals add marvelous color to a variety of dishes.

1 pound (450 g) lightly salted butter, softened
6 tablespoons (or more) chopped nasturtium flowers and
  mixed herbs
2 cups (40 g) chopped herbs (parsley works well)

1. With an electric mixer, cream the butter. Mix in the 6 tablespoons chopped nasturtium petals and mixed herbs.

2 Encase the butter in plastic wrap or parchment paper, and roll it into a cylinder. Unwrap the butter and roll it in the mixed herbs. Refrigerate until firm.

3. Slice the butter into rounds and use them to garnish and season hot dishes. Compound butters can be frozen and used later to enrich soups and sauces at the last minutes.

Roquefort Grape Clusters

1 pound (450 g) seedless grapes, red or green
8 ounces (225 g) cream cheese, softened
2 ounces (50 g) Roquefort (or other blue cheese)
8 ounces (225 g) sliced almonds, toasted and finely chopped

1. Wash and dry the grapes, and remove the stems.

2. With an electric mixer or food processor, combine the cream cheese and Roquefort until smooth.

3 Roll the grapes in the cheese mixture until coated, then roll in the chopped almonds. Chill until ready to serve.

4. Garnish with fresh grapevine.

Cold Poached Salmon With Leaves and Flowers

As good as a poached salmon tastes, it looks rather plain on a buffet. To dress it up, place it on a platter and arrange leaves and flowers over and around it. Shown here are nasturtium blooms and leaves, a feathery fern, and chives. The garnishes can simply be moved aside when time to serve.

To poach a salmon, finely chop equal amounts of carrots, onions, and celery. Add to the mixed vegetables a small handful of pickling spice. Put a layer of cheesecloth in the cavity of the cleaned salmon and pack the vegetable mixture inside. Overlap the cheesecloth and stuff the ends into the cavity, to secure the vegetable mix.

Prepare a poaching liquid of water, white wine, lemon juice, and additional pickling spice. Place the salmon in an ovenproof container and cover it with the poaching liquid; cover the container with aluminum foil. Bake at 350° F (175° C).

Check every 30 minutes with a thermometer inserted into the thickest part of the fish. When the temperature reaches 135° F (57° C), remove the container from the oven. Pour off 1/4 of the liquid and replace it with ice cubes. Put immediately into the refrigerator and allow to chill overnight in the liquid. Remove the salmon to a cooling rack placed on a baking sheet (to catch the scraps) and carefully remove the skin. Gently scrape the dark layer from the flesh and rinse with some hot poaching liquid. Transfer to a serving platter and garnish with leaves and flowers.

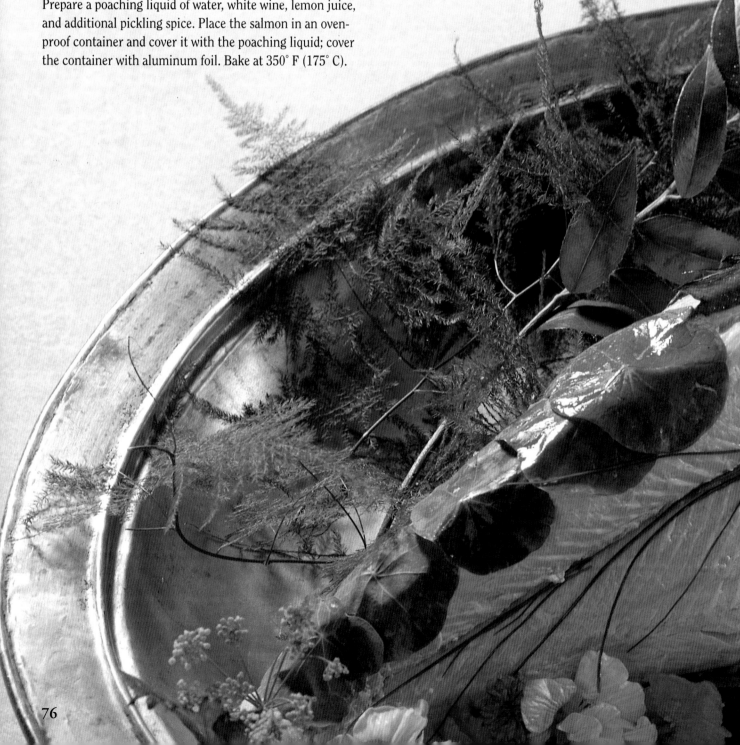

Lettuce and Flower Garnishes

Lettuce leaves, with their attractive colors and shapes, can be arranged into striking garnishes for serving platters. Examples shown, left to right, include mache leaves with enoki mushrooms; mache and Belgian endive leaves with a freesia blossom; and red lettuce with a hibiscus bloom.

A handsome herb-and-flower salad will dress up an entire meal. For the salad, use a mixture of herbs, lettuces, and flowers. Place the largest leaves on the bottom and arrange the smaller leaves and the flowers on top. The salad pictured includes arugula, mache, beet greens, tarragon, lovage, curly endive, purslane, viola flowers, chive blossoms, fennel flowers, and dill tops. Dress lightly with a balsamic vinaigrette. Combine 1 small minced shallot, 1 small minced clove of garlic, 1/4 cup (60 ml) balsamic vinegar, 1-1/2 cups (355 ml) virgin olive oil, and salt and pepper to taste. Mix well and let stand at room temperature for two to four hours.

Chocolate Cake With Pansies

For a stunning dessert, arrange a spray of brilliant pansies across any dark, smooth, chocolate cake. One way to make the glassy surface pictured here is with a chocolate ganache—an extremely thick, creamy concoction poured over a cake already frosted with butter cream. (You'll also need two chocolate cake layers made with your favorite recipe.)

BUTTER CREAM FROSTING
2 egg yolks
2/3 cup (160 ml) sifted powdered sugar
1 tablespoon vanilla
2 ounces (60 g) melted semisweet chocolate
6 ounces (1-1/2 sticks, 175 g) butter, softened

Combine all ingredients in a mixing bowl. With an electric mixer, beat at medium speed until smooth.

Frost the cake with the butter cream, so that the top is perfectly flat and the sides are smooth. Chill the cake well.

CHOCOLATE GANACHE
2 cups (500 ml) heavy cream
1-1/2 pounds (700 g) semisweet chocolate
4 ounces (120 g) unsweetened chocolate
1/4 cup (60 ml) honey

Heat all these ingredients to just below boiling, stirring constantly until velvety smooth. Allow to cool until lukewarm.

ASSEMBLY
Place the chilled, frosted cake on a screen or rack, with a pan underneath to catch the ganache. Pour the lukewarm ganache directly onto the center of the cake until the chocolate just begins to roll off the top onto the sides. With a metal spatula, smooth and push the ganache evenly over the sides. Try to do this in one turn of the spatula; the fewer strokes, the smoother the finished product. (An offset handle is helpful but not essential.) Paint in any gaps with ganache. Gently bang the pan the cake is on to further smooth the top and eliminate any bubbles. Don't try to repair anything at this stage. Let the flowers hide any flaws.

Cake With Calendula Petals

Makes one three-layer cake

Brilliant orange calendula petals and finely chopped pecans will turn a plain white cake into an event. Slice 1 to 2 cups (250–500 ml) of petals into long strips and arrange them in an attractive pattern on top. Press the chopped pecans into the sides in a scalloped pattern. While any cake with white icing will serve, the following cake shown well merits a recipe.

ITALIAN CREAM CAKE
2 cups (360 g) sugar
1-1/2 cups (350 g) butter
5 egg yolks
2 cups (240 g) flour
1 teaspoon baking soda
1 cup (250 ml) buttermilk
3 teaspoons vanilla
1/2 cup (60 g) chopped pecans
1 cup (60 g) grated coconut

1. Using an electric mixer, beat the butter until fluffy. Gradually add the sugar, beating well.

2. Add the egg yolks one at a time, beating after each one.

3. Combine flour and soda; combine buttermilk and vanilla.

4. Alternating wet and dry ingredients, add flour mixture and buttermilk mixture to the creamed butter and sugar, beginning and ending with the dry mixture.

5. Stir in pecans and coconut.

6. Beat egg whites until stiff and fold into batter.

7. Pour batter into 3 greased and floured 9-inch (22 cm) cake pans and bake at 350° F (175° C) for 25 minutes, or until golden.

CREAM CHEESE FROSTING
1/3 cup (100 g) butter, softened
8 ounces (230 g) cream cheese, softened
6-1/2 cups (520 g) sifted powdered sugar
1-1/2 teaspoons vanilla extract

1. Using an electric mixer at medium speed, beat butter and cream cheese together until creamy.

2. Gradually add powdered sugar, beating with each addition, and continue to beat until smooth.

3. Stir in vanilla extract.

Butter, Eggs, and Cheese

Temperature Control

Shaping butter is somewhat easier if it isn't rock hard. On the other hand, if it gets too warm, it becomes too soft to hold its shape. Remove it from the refrigerator 10 to 15 minutes before you begin work, and check the consistency. If it softens too much as you work with it, put it back in the refrigerator until it's the right consistency.

Butter Balls

Dip the end of a melon baller briefly in hot water. Then press it into room-temperature butter and, twisting the melon baller, scoop out balls (Figure 1). Let the butter balls cool in the refrigerator, then arrange them on a plate.

Butter Rolls

Place a stick of butter on a plate. Briefly dip the butter curler in hot water and then run it over the long side of the butter stick (Figure 2). Place the rolls in the refrigerator for a short time, then arrange them on a small plate.

Butter Cutouts

Briefly dip a large knife in hot water and then cut the butter into 1/4-inch (1/2 cm) thick slices. Use different cookie cutters and cut out various shapes (Figure 3). For a short time, put them in the refrigerator and then serve.

Butter

Molded Shapes

Butter molds, available in kitchen specialty shops, produce delightful garnishes and use up odd-sized pieces of butter. Place the mold briefly in cold water and then fill with butter that is room temperature (Figure 4), using the handle provided. Allow the shapes to harden in the refrigerator and then serve on a small plate. For different types of molds, follow the manufacturer's instructions.

Butter Rose

For four roses allow about a pound (500 g) of butter. This is a generous estimate, since there is always some waste when using a pastry bag. With a hand mixer, beat the soft butter until it is creamy and then spoon it into a pastry bag with a flat tip. Wrap a champagne cork with aluminum foil and use a needle to pin it into a firm, stable piece of fruit (e.g., an apple half). Starting at the top surface of the cork, press small petals through the pastry bag onto the cork (Figure 5). Slightly turn the cork with every petal. Always press the petals from right to left in a small, wavelike movement. Place the finished rose with its fruit base in the refrigerator until it has hardened. Then remove the rose from the cork and serve.

Butter-Curl Tree

Butter Tree

ORNAMENT OF MOLDED BUTTER

Arrange three radicchio leaves in a star shape. Place a pile of shredded orange peel in the middle and set three molded butter pieces between the radicchio leaves.

BUTTER TREE

First cut a trunk from a 1/4-inch (1/2 cm) thick slice of butter. Place the stem on a large plate. (If a dark trunk is desired, brush it with a little chicken broth.) Use a leaf-shaped cookie cutter to cut out leaves from 1/4-inch-thick (1/2 cm) slices of butter. Then arrange the leaves in a treetop and arrange a bed of sprouts at the foot of the tree.

Ornament of Molded Butter

PRETZEL FLOWER

With a pretzel cutter, cut out small pretzel shapes from 1/4-inch (1/2 cm) thick slices of butter. Place them upright on a plate and arrange them in a circle. Place a bed of sprouts in the middle.

Butter Rose

Butter Rolls in a Shell

BUTTER-CURL TREE

Using a sheet of waxed paper, roll a large piece of soft butter into a cone (Figure 6). Cut it flat at the bottom and set it upright. Dip a butter curler briefly in hot water and pull small curls off the cone from top to bottom, leaving the curls attached to the butter (Figure 7).

BUTTER ROLLS IN A SHELL

Arrange several butter rolls and balls in a large seashell.

Pretzel Flower

85

EGG SLICES

Peel a hard-boiled egg and cut slices with an egg slicer (Figure 1) or a knife. Depending on the direction of the cuts, the slices will be round or oval in shape.

EGG WEDGES

Peel a hard-boiled egg and cut wedges using an egg divider (Figure 2) or a knife.

EGG HALVES FOR STUFFING

Peel a hard-boiled egg and use a knife to cut the egg lengthwise in half (Figure 3). Remove the yolks and use for stuffing (see recipes on page 88). Rinse egg white halves under cold water, drain, and cut the bottoms flat. Using a pastry bag with a star tip, press Egg Yolk Cream (see page 13) into the egg halves (Figure 4). Or use eggs halved crosswise (Figure 5) and follow the same procedure.

CUTOUT EGG WHITE

Peel a large, hard-boiled egg and cut it into oval slices. Remove the yolks. Using small cookie cutters, cut shapes out of the egg white and arrange in ornaments.

ORNAMENT WITH EGG WHITE PIECES

Use cutout shapes from egg whites, along with red, green, and yellow bell peppers. For dark contrast pieces use purple bell peppers or pieces of truffle. Arrange the ornaments and decorate with chervil or other herb leaves.

Eggs

1

2

3

4

5

6

Garnished Egg Slice

Garnished Egg Wedges

Egg Fans

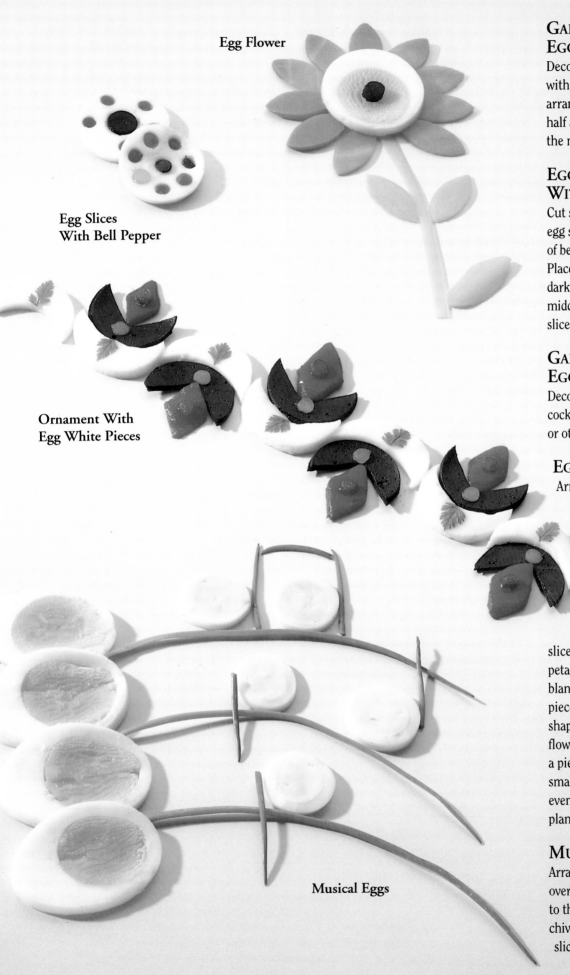

Egg Flower

**Egg Slices
With Bell Pepper**

**Ornament With
Egg White Pieces**

Musical Eggs

GARNISHED EGG SLICE

Decorate a round egg slice with stuffed olive slices arranged in a circle. Place half a cherry tomato in the middle.

EGG SLICES WITH BELL PEPPER

Cut small circles out of two egg slices and place circles of bell pepper in the holes. Place a small truffle slice or dark purple pepper in the middle. Arrange the egg slices so they overlap.

GARNISHED EGG WEDGES

Decorate egg wedges with cocktail shrimp and chervil or other herb leaves.

EGG FANS

Arrange two egg wedges, one tomato wedge, and one lemon wedge in a fan shape.

EGG FLOWER

Use one round egg slice, carrot slices cut into petal shapes, a thin strip of blanched leek, and a few pieces of leek cut into leaf shapes, and arrange as a flower. For the center use a piece of dark pepper, a small dollop of caviar, or even a small slice of eggplant skin.

MUSICAL EGGS

Arrange four oval egg slices overlapping slightly. Next to the egg slices, arrange chive stalks and quail egg slices in staff and notes.

10 hard-boiled eggs

Stuffed Eggs

Peel the eggs and halve them lengthwise. Use the egg yolks for one of the stuffings described below. Rinse the egg white halves under cold water, drain, and cut flat at the bottom so they will be stable. Prepare an egg yolk stuffing and press it into the egg white halves, using a pastry bag with a star-shaped tip.

FOR 20 EGG HALVES:
1/4 bunch fresh parsley
10 hard-boiled egg yolks
6 tablespoons mayonnaise
1/2 teaspoon mustard
Salt and white pepper

Mustard Mayonnaise Stuffing

Wash parsley, pat dry, and mince. Push the egg yolks through a fine sieve or mash with a fork until smooth. Mix the mayonnaise with the parsley, the mustard, and the egg yolks. Add salt and pepper to taste.

FOR 20 EGG HALVES:
10 hard-boiled egg yolks
4 tablespoons cottage
   cheese
2 tablespoons finely
   grated carrots
Lemon juice
2 teaspoons ground
   hazelnuts
Salt and black pepper

Carrot Nut Stuffing

Push the egg yolks through a fine sieve or mash with a fork until smooth. Blend the cottage cheese with the grated carrots, a little lemon juice, the hazelnuts, and the egg yolks. Add salt and pepper to taste.

FOR 20 EGG HALVES:
10 hard-boiled egg yolks
4 tablespoons cream
   cheese
2 tablespoons minced
   herbs
4 tablespoons milk
Salt and pepper

Herb Cheese Stuffing

Push the yolks through a fine sieve or mash with a fork until smooth. Blend the eggs well with the cheese, the herbs, and the milk, and add salt and pepper to taste.

FOR 20 EGG HALVES:
10 hard-boiled egg yolks
4 tablespoons cream
   cheese
2 tablespoons curry
   powder
2 tablespoons avocado
   puree*
2 teaspoons lemon juice
2 tablespoons milk
Salt and pepper

Curried Avocado Stuffing

Note: Ripe avocado pieces can be pureed in a food processor or simply mashed thoroughly with a fork until smooth.

Push the egg yolks through a fine sieve or mash with a fork until smooth. Then blend well with the cheese, curry powder, avocado puree, lemon juice, and milk. Add salt and pepper to taste.

EGGS IN A NEST
Using sprouts and finely grated or julienned carrots, make two circles. Place two peeled and halved quail eggs in the circle and one whole, half-peeled quail egg in the middle.

EGG HALF WITH CARROT-NUT STUFFING
Decorate the stuffing with radish slices, cucumber pieces, carrot strips, and a hazelnut.

HERB CHEESE STUFFING
Decorate with herb leaves, a piece of cheese, and a ring of bell pepper.

MUSTARD MAYONNAISE STUFFING
Decorate the stuffing with tomato strips and herb leaves.

AVOCADO STUFFING
Decorate with bell pepper pieces, truffle, herb leaves, and pieces of carrot.

EGG TEACUP
Cut a lid off the top of a hard-boiled egg and cut it flat at the bottom. Remove the yolk. Fill the hole with green gelatin and allow it to harden in the refrigerator. Place the egg half on a fluted cucumber slice. For the handle, insert a piece of pretzel in the side of the egg. Decorate the cup with a diamond-shaped piece of bell pepper and a chervil or other herb leaf.

Quail Eggs in Nest

Egg Teacup

Herb Cheese Stuffing

Carrot-Nut Stuffing

Curried Avocado Stuffing

Mustard Mayonnaise Stuffing

89

VARIETIES

For garnishings such as small skewers or cheese cutouts, hard and sliced cheeses (for example Emmenthaler, Gruyere, Cheddar, Gouda, and Edam) are best, since they have a firm texture. If possible, remove cheese from the refrigerator an hour before serving, so its aroma can develop.

CHEESE SLICES

Hard cheese can be easily cut into even slices with a special cheese slicer or a cutting wire (Figure 1). Slices look attractive when they are cut with a fluted knife (Figure 2).

CHEESE CUTOUTS

First cut a block of cheese (Emmenthaler, Gouda, Edam, Gruyere) into 1/2-inch (1 cm) thick slices, using a knife or a cutting wire. Then cut out different shapes with cookie cutters.

CHEESE BLOSSOMS

Blossoms require a small (about 1-pound, or 500 g) piece of semihard cheese in a cylindrical shape. The cheese shown is a fragrant type known as Tête-de-Moine. First cut a lid off the top. Then pierce the pin of a girolle (a special cutting tool for this type of cheese) through the middle of it, put the shaving knife in place, and, by turning the knife, shave off small, thin cheese blossoms (Figure 4). When finished, always cover the cheese, using the removed lid.

Cheese

CHEESE BOATS

Pierce one end of a bell pepper slice with a garnishing pick. Stick the pick through a stuffed olive, then through the other end of the bell pepper. Insert the pick in a slice of cheese (Edam or Gouda) that has been cut into a flower shape.

Girolle With Tête-de-Moine Blossoms

90

FIR TREE KEBAB

Use a 1/2-inch (1 cm) thick slice of Edam or Gruyere. Using cookie cutters, cut one large and two small fir trees. Spread butter on the edge of a round pumpernickel slice and roll it in minced parsley. Place the cheese fir trees on the bread and fasten with picks.

CHEESE WINDMILL

Cut out small oval shapes from 1/2-inch (1 cm) thick slices of Tilsit, Edam, Emmenthaler, and Gruyere cheese. Dip the edges in sweet paprika and minced parsley. Then place them on a pumpernickel slice covered with cream cheese. Place a red grape half on top.

COLORFUL CHEESE KEBAB

Cut out three different shapes and sizes of cheese and stack them on top of each other, from large to small. With a wooden pick, skewer one green and one red grape and a stuffed olive, and stick the pick through the cheese slices.

RHOMBOID PICKS

Stick a red grape and a rhomboid cheese motif on a wooden pick and place it into a circle of Edam and pumpernickel.

Fir Tree Kabobs

Cheese Windmill

Rhomboid Picks

Colorful Cheese Kabob

Cheese Boats

Cold Comfort

Sugar or Salt Rims

Pour sugar or salt into a small, flat bowl. Cut into a lemon slice, place it on the glass, and run it around the edge (Figure 1). Remove the lemon. (Alternatively, dip the glass upside down in a flat bowl with lemon juice and then into the sugar or salt.) Carefully tap the glass to shake off loose granules, and let dry. To make colorful edges, first dip the glass edge in colored liqueur and then in sugar. Or drizzle the sugar with liqueur and dip a glass whose edge has been dipped in lemon juice into the sugar (Figures 2 and 3).

Lemon Hexagon

Cut the peel from a lemon slice in six cuts to form a hexagon (Figure 4). Make a cut into the center and place on a glass.

Drink Decorations

Peel Spirals

For a thin spiral, use a peel stripper and cut the peel of a citrus fruit (orange, lemon, or lime) in a spiral (Figure 5). For a wider spiral, use a knife to remove the peel. Position one end of the spiral in the glass and the other, longer end outside.

Fruit Slices

Cut from the peel to the center (Figure 6), and place in glass.

Opposite Page

1. Cocktail cherry on a cocktail pick, and lemon hexagon.
2. Slice of lime, lime spiral, and cocktail cherry.
3. Half an orange slice, lime spiral, and star fruit slice.
4. Quarter of a pineapple slice and a kebab with two cocktail cherries.
5. Slice of lime and mint sprig.
6. Half an orange slice, pineapple leaf, and long orange peel spiral.
7. Quarter of a pineapple slice, cocktail cherry on a pick, and mint sprig.
8. Melon wedge and lily blossom.

Kebabs

Skewer fruit pieces or slices on small kebabs and lay them across the glass. Place larger kebabs in the glass.

94

1

2

3

4

5

6

7

8

VODKA BOTTLE WITH HEATHER AND MINT

Vodka's resistance to freezing allows for a show-stopping garnish—and very cold drinks.

Select a nonporous, freezer-safe container that is slightly larger than a bottle of your favorite vodka. Spray the inside of the container lightly with oil or nonstick cooking spray.

Tape or glue strands of heather and sprigs of mint to the vodka bottle. Place the bottle in the center of the container and add water up to the bottle's neck. Place upright in the freezer and freeze overnight. Unmold by running warm water over the container, and serve immediately.

Fire and Ice Sorbet

2 cups (360 g) sugar
2 cups (500 ml) water
1 cup (250 ml) fresh lime juice
1 teaspoon finely diced fresh jalapeno pepper
1 tablespoon finely diced mild red pepper
Small red pepper
Lime slice

1. Combine sugar and water in a medium saucepan and simmer until sugar dissolves. Cool to room temperature, then cover and refrigerate.

2. Combine remaining ingredients and allow to sit at room temperature for several hours.

3. Add pepper-lime juice mixture to cold syrup and freeze according to your ice-cream maker's specifications.

4. Garnish with small red pepper and lime slice.

ICE CUBES WITH EDIBLE FLOWERS

Place edible flowers and leaves in each compartment of ice cube trays, using a variety of colors, if possible. Fill with water and freeze overnight.

Sauces

Sauces are spectacular garnishes. These smooth, colorful mixtures can be placed on top of food (for example, green pesto dribbled over tomato-sauced manicotti). Dollops of sauce can be placed next to the food. Another option is to spoon a sauce over part of the plate—or all of it—and rest the food on top.

Coulis

"Coulis" is a general term referring to a very thick sauce or puree. Originally, the term was used to describe the juices from cooked meat. At left, a grilled filet mignon rests on Pickled Pumpkin Coulis, further garnished with rosemary and dollops of Tomatillo Coulis. In the center, Cranberry Orange Coulis is shown with a roast quail, pieces of pickled pumpkin, and slivers of lime peel. At right, Southwest Tomatillo Coulis garnishes stuffed prawns, with a few added rose petals.

PICKLED PUMPKIN COULIS

Dice 2 cups (400 g) raw pumpkin. In a medium saucepan, combine pumpkin with 1 cup (200 g) sugar, 2/3 cup (160 ml) white vinegar, and a pinch each of salt, whole mustard seeds, and white pepper. Simmer until pumpkin is tender, and process in a blender or food processor until smooth.

CRANBERRY ORANGE COULIS

Combine 1 cup (200 g) sugar, 1 cup (250 ml) water, and the chopped zest of 1 orange. Simmer for 10 to 15 minutes. Add one 12-ounce (350 g) package of cranberries, rinsed and sorted. Cook for 10 minutes until berries split. Allow to cool slightly. In food processor or blender, process with 2 ounces (50 g) of butter until the berries are well chopped but not totally pureed.

SOUTHWEST TOMATILLO COULIS

Peel and coarsely dice 12 tomatillos. Finely chop 3 garlic cloves. Rough-cut 1/4 cup (1/2 g) fresh cilantro. In a small saucepan, saute all ingredients in a little oil for 5 minutes. Add a pinch each of salt, cumin, cayenne, and oregano. Add 1 cup (250 ml) white wine and simmer 15 minutes. Allow to cool slightly. In a food processor or blender, process with 2 ounces (50 g) of butter until well minced but not totally pureed.

Purees

At left, Ruby Port Sauce, intended to garnish fish, is shown decorated with a few dollops of Pumpkin Coulis (see page 100). A table knife was pulled through the orange coulis to create the design. In the center, Roasted Pepper Purees—both red and green—dress up grilled scallops. At right, a few drops of sour cream and an herb grouping add to the Roasted Red Pepper Puree. (To make the sour cream hearts, drop five small dollops of sour cream onto the puree and pull a kitchen knife through the centers of the dots.)

RUBY PORT SAUCE

In a food processor, finely chop 2 cups (350 g) Ruby-Flame grapes (red seedless grapes). Place in a saucepan with 2 cups (500 ml) port wine and bring to a boil. Add a pinch of salt and 1 teaspoon sugar. Reduce this mixture by 3/4. Add 1 quart (1 l) of fish stock and again reduce by 1/2. Adjust seasoning if necessary. Strain well through a fine sieve. This should not need any additional thickening if reduced to the correct consistency.

ROASTED PEPPER SAUCE

To make a red puree, use red bell peppers; to make a green puree, use green bell peppers.

Roast 4 bell peppers until the skin turns black. This can be done by spearing each pepper on a wooden-handled fork and holding it over an open flame or electric burner; or the peppers can be placed under a broiler, close to the heat. Immerse the blackened peppers in ice water and peel off the charred skin, scraping any remnants off with a knife. Remove the stems, seeds, and ribs.

Roughly dice the peppers and place in a saucepan with 1 finely diced shallot and 1 cup (250 ml) Zinfandel wine (or other full-bodied red wine). Simmer until the wine evaporates, then add 3 cups (750 ml) of chicken stock and 1/4 teaspoon salt. Reduce this by 1/2 and puree in the blender with 2 ounces (60 g) butter or margarine. Be creative with the seasoning. This process works for all the colors of bell peppers you can find.

Creams

A snow-white sauce is an arresting garnish for an entree that boasts abundant color of its own. At left, triangles of Lemon Yogurt Cream Sauce sit atop Roasted Green Pepper Puree (see page 102). In this case, the garnished entree is a handsome vegetable jardiniere—chopped vegetables baked in phyllo dough—but any interesting entree would do. In the center, Curried Crème Fraîche provides a colorful backdrop for crab relish and an oriental noodle cake. At right, a creamy Sauce Newburg, perfect for a variety of entrees, is further decorated with dill flowers and sour cream. To make the sour cream pattern, add a large dollop and pull a kitchen knife toward, then away from, the center.

WARM LEMON YOGURT CREAM SAUCE

Bring to a boil 1 cup (250 ml) of chicken stock. Add the juice and zest of 1 lemon. Make a slurry of 1 tablespoon cornstarch and 1 tablespoon water, add to the sauce, and stir to thicken. Whip in 1-1/2 cups (360 ml) yogurt, 1 teaspoon poppy seeds, and 1 teaspoon chopped chives. Season with salt and pepper.

CURRIED CREME FRAICHE

Reduce 1 cup (250 ml) white wine, the juice of 1 lime, 1 finely chopped shallot, and 1/4 teaspoon chopped ginger in a saucepan until syrupy. Add 4 cups (1 l) crème fraîche (or 3 cups heavy cream and 1 cup sour cream). Add 1 tablespoon curry powder and a pinch of salt. Bring to a boil, lower heat, and simmer to desired consistency.

SAUCE NEWBURG

Melt 2 tablespoons butter in a saucepan and stir in 2 tablespoons flour. Stir over low heat for 5 minutes. Slowly whisk in 2 cups (500 ml) milk. Add salt and white pepper to taste. Add 1 teaspoon paprika and 1/2 cup (120 ml) good-quality, pale dry sherry. Continue to stir until mixture just reaches the boiling point, but do not boil. Remove from heat and strain in fine-mesh strainer. Top with a pat of butter.

Oils

If an empty plate is a canvas, flavored and colored oils are paints. They can be splattered on with expressionist flair, brushed on for a more traditional result, or applied in almost oriental flourishes with plastic squirt bottles. At left, Yellow Pepper Wasabi Oil decorates sliced, grilled venison. (A grilled scallop, rosemary tips, and radish slices complete the plate.) In the center, Green Pepper and Cilantro Oil mixes with Garlic Basil Oil to garnish a broiled filet, further dressed with fresh herbs. At right, a thin film of Garlic Basil Oil is ready for an entree.

YELLOW PEPPER WASABI OIL

Juice 4 yellow bell peppers, place the juice in a small saucepan, and cook over medium heat until reduced to 1/4 its original volume. Stir in 1 teaspoon each wasabi powder (oriental horseradish) and rice wine vinegar. Add 2 cups (500 ml) olive oil and shake well. Allow the oil to sit for two days, shaking periodically to combine.

JUICING PEPPERS

The easiest way to juice peppers is in a juicer, following the manufacturer's instructions. In its absence, cut the peppers into quarters, removing all seeds and ribs. Bring 1/4 cup (60 ml) water to a boil in a small saucepan, add peppers, and cover tightly. Reduce the heat to low and steam the peppers for 10 to 15 minutes, or until the water is almost evaporated. Allow to cool to room temperature. To extract the juice, wring the peppers in cheesecloth or press them through a very fine-mesh sieve.

GREEN PEPPER AND CILANTRO OIL

Juice 4 green bell peppers with 1/2 cup (1 g) fresh cilantro, place the juice mixture in a small saucepan, and cook over medium heat until reduced to 1/4 its original volume. Add 2 cups (500 ml) olive oil and shake well. Allow the oil to sit for two days, shaking periodically to combine.

Garlic Basil Oil

1/4 cup (40 g) garlic cloves
1 cup (2 g) packed basil leaves
2 cups (500 ml) olive oil
1 cup (100 g) mixed red and yellow
 pepper strips
  cut 1/2 inch (1 cm) long

Peel and juice 1/4 cup garlic cloves with 1 cup packed basil leaves. Add 2 cups olive oil and allow to stand overnight. Prepare 1 cup mixed red and yellow bell pepper strips, cut 1/2 inch long. Trim off and discard the inside flesh, leaving only the outer skins. Add the strips of pepper skin to the oil and allow to stand overnight.

107

Dessert Sauces

At left, a creamy White Dessert Sauce With Raspberry Hearts is a gorgeous base for any dessert. In the center, Passion Fruit Sauce adds color to a pale frozen mousse. At right, Spider Web Chocolate Sauce provides striking color contrasts.

White Dessert Sauce With Raspberry Hearts

3/4 cup (130 g) sugar	2 cups (500 ml) milk
1 ounce (30 g) cornstarch	2 cups (500 ml) cream
2 eggs	Vanilla bean

Combine sugar and cornstarch in a stainless steel bowl. Add eggs and whip to combine well. Heat the milk and cream with the vanilla bean to just before the boiling point. Add a little hot milk mixture to the egg mixture, then combine both mixtures and return them to the stove. Heat to boiling, whisking constantly with a wire whip. Strain and cool. Cover a plate with white dessert sauce. Place evenly spaced dots of raspberry sauce in a circle around the edge of the white sauce, spiraling in slightly to the center of the plate. Pull a toothpick through the middle of each dot to form the hearts.

RASPBERRY SAUCE

Combine 6 cups (1-1/2 l) frozen, unsweetened raspberries and 1-1/2 cups (360 g) sugar, and cook over medium heat until sugar is dissolved. Do not boil. Strain through fine-meshed sieve and refrigerate.

Passion Fruit Sauce

2 cups (500 ml) passion fruit puree, divided
2 tablespoons cornstarch
3/4 cup (130 g) sugar

Combine 1/4 cup (60 ml) of the passion fruit puree with the cornstarch, to make a slurry for thickening. Heat remaining puree and sugar, stirring to dissolve sugar. Add slurry and cook until thickened. Refrigerate. To make the patterns, start with passion fruit sauce on the plate. Pour raspberry sauce into a plastic squeeze bottle and squeeze two or three lines of it across the passion fruit. With a toothpick or small skewer, draw through the lines in a steady S design, leaving the skewer on the plate until you come to the end of the line.

Spider Web Mocha Sauce

Hot, brewed coffee
1 cup (70 g) cocoa
1/4 cup (45 g) sugar
1/2 cup (120 ml) light corn syrup

Make a stiff paste with the hot coffee and cocoa, whisking out all lumps. Add a little more coffee to form a thick syrup. Dissolve sugar in coffee mixture and add corn syrup. Use the sauce either room temperature or chilled. If the sauce is too thick, add a little water. To create the design, start with mocha sauce on the plate. Place some white dessert sauce in a plastic bottle and squeeze two lines of it across the chocolate. Using a toothpick, pull across the lines, then pull across the lines in the opposite direction. Repeat at even intervals all the way across the white lines.

Sweet Talk

Although most of the ingredients in this chapter are familiar to everyone, a few hints might prove helpful.

MELTING CHOCOLATE

Chocolate, even good-quality baking chocolate, scorches easily. When it does, it turns bitter and loses much of its rich flavor and aroma. To avoid burning it, break the chocolate into reasonably small pieces and place them in the top of a double boiler over hot water. Stir the melting chocolate constantly, to avoid sticking and overheating. If you don't have a double boiler, place a metal bowl or small pan inside a larger pan of hot water.

PREPARING MARZIPAN

Marzipan dough is available in well-stocked groceries, usually in rolls wrapped in plastic. A mixture of ground almonds and sugar, it can often be unwrapped and used immediately. Also available is canned almond paste. While it is likewise a mixture of almonds and sugar, it is much too sticky to be used as is. Break the paste into chunks in a mixing bowl. For an 8-ounce (237 g) can of paste, add about 1 cup (80 g) of powdered sugar and knead the two together until mixed. Turn the dough out onto a work surface that has been dusted with powdered sugar to prevent sticking, and knead in 1 to 1-1/2 cups (80 to 120 g) more powdered sugar. The dough should be pliable and easy to work with. Check the package label for further instructions. In any case, check the texture of the dough. Add powdered sugar if it is too sticky, a little water if it is too dry, and knead until pliable.

To tint marzipan different colors, use cocoa powder or food coloring. Flatten the prepared marzipan into a disk with the heel of your hand, place the cocoa or food coloring in the center, and fold up the sides. Knead the marzipan until the color is evenly distributed.

Exposed to the air, marzipan dries out quickly and becomes difficult to work with, so prepare only as much as you are going to use. When it dries, it holds the shape it has been molded, rolled, and/or cut into.

MOLDING WITH MARZIPAN

To mold small figures, use marzipan dough, kneaded with powdered sugar if necessary, and dyed different colors (see page 122), depending on the figure. First mold the marzipan, using your hands, into the basic shapes of the figure. Then glue the parts together with sugar glaze—powdered sugar moistened with water to form a medium-thick liquid (see page 126). Make sure the figure has a firm stand (possibly flatten the bottom slightly) and doesn't lean to one side.

GLACEED FLOWERS

With a fork or wire whisk, beat an egg white until it is well mixed but not frothy. Using a fine brush, paint the front and back of the flowers with egg white. Place the flowers on a bed of superfine sugar and sprinkle the tops with more sugar. Touch up any blank spaces with more egg white and sugar. Let the flowers dry in an airy place. If the weather is damp, place them in a 300° F (150° C) oven for 10 minutes.

CRYSTALLIZED GINGER AND CITRUS PEEL

Boil 1 cup (180 g) sugar and 1 cup (250 ml) water for 10 minutes. Add peeled, sliced ginger or julienned strips of lemon, lime, or orange rind from which the white pith has been completely removed. Boil until the strips are tender and have turned translucent. Remove from the syrup and drain on waxed paper. If extra sweetness is desired, sprinkle the peel or ginger with superfine sugar.

SPREADING CHOCOLATE

Pour melted chocolate onto a smooth sheet of parchment paper or waxed paper, and spread it with a frosting knife or a spatula, about 1/8 inch (2 to 3 mm) thick. Allow the chocolate to cool and harden slightly, but not completely, so that it won't break when pressed or cut out.

CHOCOLATE CUTOUTS

Spread the chocolate as described above. Dip a knife briefly in hot water and then cut out the shapes—diamonds, squares, and rectangles, for example (Figure 1). Allow the chocolate to cool. Lift the shapes off the paper with a spatula, and let them harden completely on another sheet of paper. To cut out different shapes with cookie cutters (Figure 2), dip the cutters in hot water before using.

CHOCOLATE ROLLS

With a spatula or frosting knife, spread the heated chocolate thinly on a marble board. Allow the chocolate to cool until it's semihardened. Place a spatula flat against one edge and push it forward 6 to 8 inches (2 to 3 cm). The pushing movement curls the chocolate into small rolls (Figure 3).

Chocolate

CHOCOLATE FANS

Place a spatula flat against one edge of semihard spread chocolate (see Chocolate Rolls). Push the spatula forward for about 5 inches (2 cm) but hold down one end of the chocolate so it curls into the shape of a fan (Figure 4).

CHOCOLATE LEAVES

Set aside melted chocolate in a bowl. Carefully wash small, smooth leaves with stems (rose leaves, birch leaves, and such) and pat dry. Holding a leaf by the stem, pull the top surface through the chocolate. Scrape excess chocolate off on the edge of the bowl and place leaves, chocolate side up, on a sheet of parchment paper or waxed paper. Allow chocolate to harden completely on the leaf in a cool place. Then carefully pull the leaf away from the chocolate (Figure 5).

CHOCOLATE TART SHELLS

Wash and dry a metal tart cup and allow it to cool. Fill the cup to the brim with heated chocolate and immediately pour it out again. Use a knife to scrape off the excess chocolate that formed at the rim during pouring. Repeat with additional cups. Place the cups in the refrigerator until the chocolate has hardened (Figure 6). Then use a knife to carefully remove the chocolate from the cup and fill as desired.

Chocolate Boxes

Chocolate Fans

Chocolate Ornaments

Chocolate Rolls

CHOCOLATE ORNAMENTS

Use cutout shapes of chocolate and marzipan (see page 122) to arrange different ornaments.

CHOCOLATE BOXES

For each box, cut three 1-inch (3 cm) squares from semisweet chocolate and two 1-inch squares from white chocolate. Glue the squares into a box with sugar glaze (see page 126) and let it harden. Fill box with whipped cream and garnish with a piece of strawberry and a mint leaf.

115

MAKING AND FILLING A PASTRY CONE

Fold a square sheet of waxed paper, about 6 x 6 inches (15 x 15 cm) in size, diagonally into a triangle and cut at the fold. Use one triangle per bag (Figure 1). Starting with a short side, roll up the triangle into a cone (Figure 2) with its tip closed (Figure 3). Place the cone tip-down into the neck of a bottle so it stays upright, and then half-fill with melted chocolate. Now fold the highest paper corner at the open end toward the front. Then fold in the corners toward the middle and slowly roll the fold down (Figure 5), until there is slight pressure on the filling.

MAKING FILIGREE ORNAMENTS

Draw the ornaments with a black felt-tip pen on a sheet of white paper and place thin waxed paper over it (Figure 4). Fill the homemade pastry cone with melted chocolate, as described above, and use scissors to cut off the tip in the desired size (Figure 5). With a very small hole, the motifs will be more delicate.

Hold the cone in the left hand and exert pressure with the right hand. (Do the reverse if you're left-handed.) Trace over the drawn ornaments with the cone tip, gently squeezing the chocolate onto the paper as you go. Try for even pressure and a steady hand. Don't hold the cone too close to the paper, or you won't be able to see the shape.

116

Chocolate Motifs

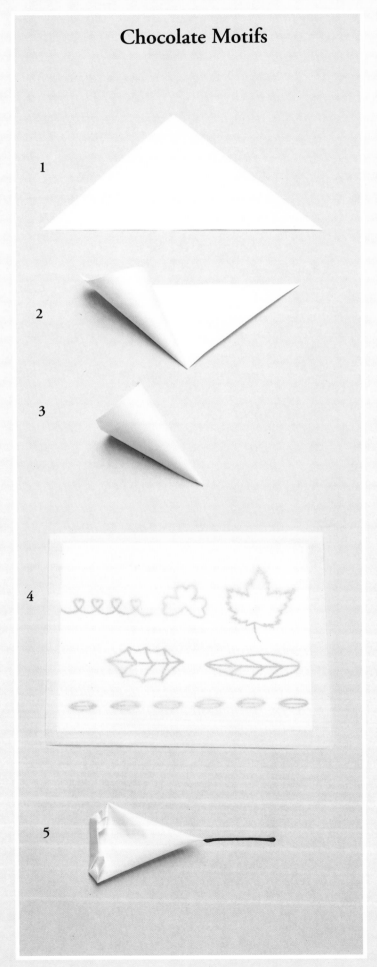

1

2

3

4

5

Allow the finished ornaments to cool completely, then carefully lift them off the paper, using a sharp knife. It is possible to prepare these ornaments far in advance, ready for decorating cakes, petit fours, or other desserts. Store them in layers separated by waxed paper in a tightly sealed plastic container in a cool place. They will keep three to four weeks.

Small desserts look very pretty when served on plates that have been dusted with powdered sugar or cocoa powder, using stencils and a fine sieve. The same technique can be used to decorate cakes (see page 120). For patterns with powdered sugar, use dark plates, and for patterns with cocoa, use light-colored plates. The plates should be large and have a flat rim (possibly without patterns). It is important not to dust all around the rim, because the pattern would be destroyed when serving. It is better to leave a corner or even half of the rim undusted.

SMALL STENCILS

Draw the desired shape (for example, a star) on a piece of stiff, white paper and cut it out. Then cut the entire stencil into a spoon shape, to provide a long handle for lifting (Figure 1). The cocoa droplets that encircle the plate at the bottom of the opposite page used just such a stencil.

Plates With Powdered Sugar and Cocoa

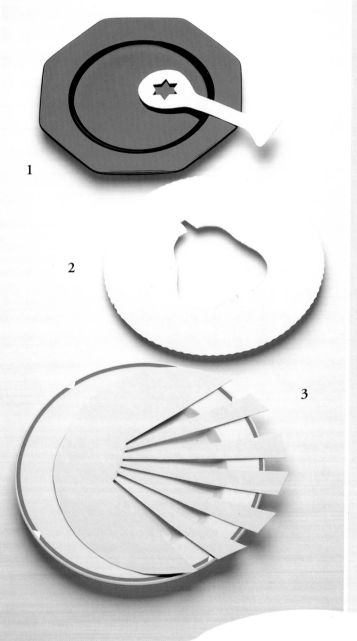

1

2

3

Plate With Star

LARGER STENCILS

Larger stencils cover the whole plate (see Figure 2). The pattern is usually centered on the plate and the dessert is then placed on top. Large stencils are easy to hold on to and thus don't need a handle. To remove a large stencil, grasp it with both hands on opposite sides and carefully lift it off. The star at the bottom of this page and the flower on the opposite page were created with plate-size stencils.

STRIPED PATTERN

Using thin cardboard, cut the stencil shown in Figure 3. Lay it on the plate and dust it with cocoa or powdered sugar.

PLATE WITH CHAMPAGNE GLASS AND STARS

Dust the cocoa stars on the plate as described for Figure 1. Make a stencil for the champagne glass, also as described for Figure 1, and dust it with cocoa powder. Then carefully fill the inside of the glass with powdered sugar, using a spoon. Correct the borders with a knife, if necessary.

118

**Plate With Stars
and Champagne Glass**

Plate With Flower

**Plate With Striped
Pattern**

Plate With Drops

119

MAKING STENCILS

Cakes can be left free of frosting and decorated instead with powdered sugar or cocoa, depending or the color of the cake. Frosted cakes can be made even more attractive with the same materials. The only requirements are powdered sugar or cocoa powder, a fine sieve, and homemade stencils.

Stencils should always be cut from stiff paper (Figure 1), so they won't bend and destroy the pattern when lifted off. With smaller stencils, attach small handles for lifting. For the handle, cut a strip of paper about 2 inches (5 cm) wide and 4 inches (10 cm) long. Fold it in the middle, then fold under each end (Figure 2) and glue the handle to the middle of the stencil (Figure 3). The handle shouldn't unbalance the stencil. For a larger stencil, attach two handles on opposite sides.

STRIPED OR CHECKED PATTERN

You'll need strips of paper between 2-1/2 and 3 inches (6 and 8 cm) wide and about 4 inches (10 cm) longer than the cake. Handles are not necessary. Lay the paper strips either parallel or crosswise on the cake, leaving 2 inches (5 cm) on each side. Depending on the color of the cake, use either powdered sugar or cocoa and sift it onto the surface, covering the whole cake. Then take both ends of the paper strips and carefully lift them straight up off the cake.

Cakes With Cocoa and Powdered Sugar

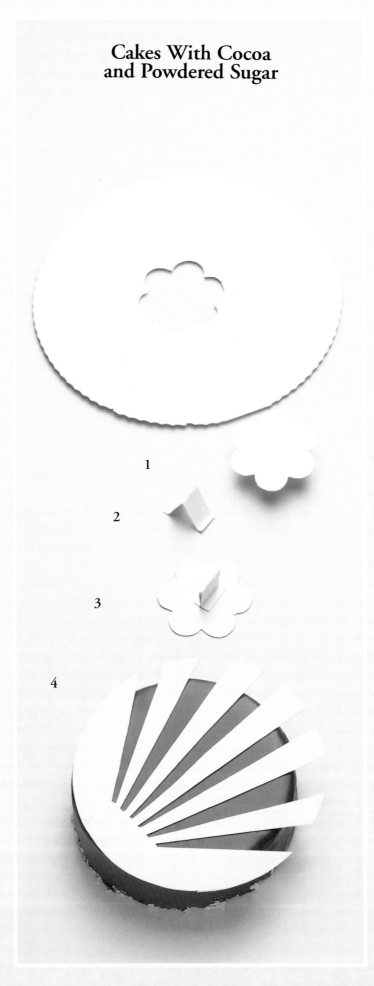

1

2

3

4

FAN PATTERN

Using thin cardboard, cut the stencil shown in Figure 4. Lay it on a round cake and dust it with powdered sugar or cocoa. Then carefully lift the stencil, using both hands.

CHECKED CAKE

Lay several paper strips crosswise on a square cake with dark chocolate icing, or on a chocolate cake that has not been iced. Dust it with powdered sugar and carefully remove each strip.

CAKE WITH APPLE AND CUPID'S ARROW

Using stiff paper or thin cardboard, cut out an apple stencil. Attach a handle in the middle. Lay the stencil on a heart-shaped cake that has been iced with white icing. Sift cocoa powder on the surface and carefully lift off the stencil. Garnish the lower edge of the cake and the apple with pink marzipan (see page 122). Using a pastry bag, squeeze small rosettes of chocolate icing around the upper edge of the cake. If desired, add purchased icing flowers and pistachio nuts.

CAKE WITH STAR PATTERN

Cut out a large star in the center of a round piece of thin cardboard about 12 inches (30 cm) in diameter. Lay the stencil on a cake covered with marzipan (see page 126) or with a smooth, firm, light-colored frosting. Dust the stencil with cocoa and lift it off. Cut a small

star in the center of a second piece of round, 12-inch-diameter cardboard. Hold it over the cake, close to the surface but not touching, and dust it with powdered sugar. Decorate the cake edges with melted chocolate (see page 116).

Cake With Star

Cake With Checked Pattern

Cake With Apple and Cupid's Arrow

ROLLING MARZIPAN

Use a rolling pin to roll out prepared marzipan about 1/8 to 1/4 inch (4 to 5 mm) thick (Figure 1). Dust your work surface with powdered sugar first.

MARZIPAN CUTOUTS

Use small cookie cutters to cut out different shapes from rolled-out marzipan (Figure 2).

MARZIPAN MOTIFS

Use this technique for larger shapes for which you have no cutters. First draw the motif on thin cardboard and cut it out. Then place the pattern on the rolled-out marzipan (Figure 3), and cut out the motif with a small knife. Lift it off the work surface with a wide spatula.

MARZIPAN CUPS

Roll the marzipan about 1/8 inch (4 mm) thick and press out a circle, using a round, smooth or ridged cutter about 2 inches (5 cm) in diameter. Make a cut from the edge to the middle (Figure 4) and press the edges together so the marzipan is shaped like a small cup (Figure 5).

DICE

Roll out the marzipan about 1/2 inch (1 cm) thick. Cut off 1/2-inch-wide strips (Figure 6). From the strips, cut off small cubes 1/2 inch long (Figure 7). For the dots, press in small bits of chocolate.

Marzipan

HORSESHOES

Roll the marzipan into a piece 1/4 inch (6 mm) thick, and cut off a strip 1/2 inch (1 cm) wide and 4 inches (10 cm) long. Bend the strip into the shape of a horseshoe. Shape the ends and the middle piece (Figure 8). Press on small dots of baking chocolate.

NUMBERS AND LETTERS

Roll the marzipan 1/8 inch (3 mm) thick. With a smooth pastry wheel, cut 1/4-inch (6 mm) wide strips and place them upright (Figure 9). Form letters or numbers (Figure 10). Stencils can be helpful.

Ornaments From Cutout Marzipan

Ornament of Marzipan Cups

ORNAMENTS

Dye marzipan different colors and roll out pieces 1/8 inch (3 mm) thick. Cut out different shapes with cookie cutters. Combine them to form ornaments and decorate with melted chocolate if desired (see page 116).

FLOWER BOUQUET

Roll out 1/4-inch (3 mm) thick marzipan that has been dyed in three different colors. Press out the necessary shapes using stencils and small cutters. Arrange them to form a vase with flowers. Preserved strips of angelica can serve as stems.

MEADOW

Prepare in the same way as the vase with flowers.

CUP ORNAMENT

Press out three ridged circles from marzipan that has been rolled 1/8 inch (3 mm) thick. With a knife, score star-shaped lines. Cut the circles once to the middle and shape them into cups. Place a marzipan ball in the middle. Roll out marzipan that was dyed with cocoa into a 1/8-inch (3 mm) thick piece and cut out an elliptical shape. Place the cups on top. Decorate with marzipan leaves. Then roll green-dyed marzipan into small balls and arrange them around the cups.

Flower Bouquet With Vase

Marzipan Meadow

MARZIPAN PEAR

Roll a 3-ounce (80 g) piece of marzipan into a ball (Figure 1). Use more or less dough, depending on the size you want. Then shape the ball into a pear and punch a notch in the bottom with a skewer or an awl (Figure 2). Place a small, brown piece of marzipan in the hole. For the stem, use a piece of angelica or a piece of green-tinted marzipan. You can paint it with food coloring diluted with water, using an ordinary paint brush.

MARZIPAN APPLE

Prepare in the same way as the pear, but use the marzipan ball as the basic shape.

MUSHROOM

Roll a small piece of marzipan into a cylinder and shape the mushroom stem (Figure 3). Then roll red marzipan into a ball, cut it in half with a knife, and indent one half on the cut side slightly with a knife. Make tiny balls from white marzipan, flatten them, and press them onto the mushroom head (Figure 4), using a mixture of powdered sugar and water for the glue. Place the mushroom cap on top of the stem and glue the two parts together.

MARZIPAN ANGEL

For the body, make a pear-shaped marzipan piece and punch a hole in the front (Figure 5). Shape the head from a ball (Figure 6) and the mouth from a smaller

Marzipan

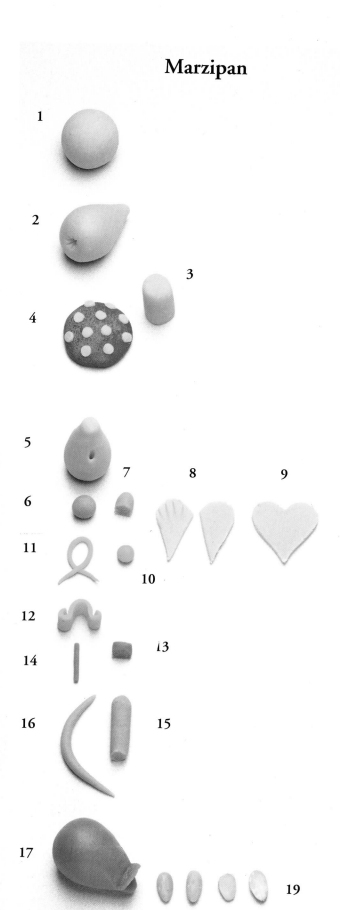

ball (Figure 7). Make a small dent in the mouth with a toothpick or small skewer. Make the wings (Figure 8) from a cutout heart (Figure 9). For the neck scarf, roll a small ball (Figure 10) into a string (Figure 11). Shape the hair from a narrow strip (Figure 12). For the candle, use pink marzipan (Figure 13) shaped into a thin roll (Figure 14), and make the arms (Figure 16) from a thicker roll (Figure 15). Assemble all the parts into an angel, as shown in the photo, and press on eyes made from sugar glaze and chocolate.

MARZIPAN PIGLET

Form a 3-ounce (80 g) piece of marzipan into a pear shape. Slightly flatten the narrow top, make one small incision, and form the snout (Figure 17). For the tail, roll a small piece of marzipan into a thin roll, with one side ending in a tip, and twist it into a curlicue (Figure 18). Fasten it to the piglet. Use four peeled and halved almonds (Figure 19) for ears and feet, and sugar glaze and chocolate for eyes.

MARZIPAN BUNNY

For the head, make one cut down into the narrow end of a teardrop-shaped piece of marzipan, and place it on top of a large ball. For arms and legs, use thin cylinders; for the tail, use a small ball. Fasten the parts to the body and press on a face made from chocolate bits.

MARZIPAN HARE

For the head, make one cut down into the narrow end of a teardrop-shaped marzipan piece. For the body, cut halfway into one end of a thick roll and shape the

Marzipan Angel

Marzipan Mushroom in a Garden

Marzipan Hare

Marzipan Piglets

Marzipan Horseshoe

Marzipan Apple

Marzipan Pear

two end pieces into legs. Place the head on top on the body. Press on a face made from chocolate bits.

MUSHROOM GARDEN

Press a circle out of chocolate (see page 114) and place a marzipan mushroom on top. For the moss, arrange green marzipan that was pushed through a fine sieve. Use green marzipan to make thin cylinders with your hands, cut them in small pieces, and bend the pieces into arches. Use sugar glaze to attach them like fence posts to the base.

Marzipan Bunny

Marzipan Dice

MAKING GLAZE

Place powdered sugar in a mixing bowl and gradually add warm water, stirring constantly, until the sugar is dissolved and the glaze is the desired consistency. A glaze that will be spread with a knife should be thicker than one into which small items will be dipped.

APPLYING GLAZE

Apply sugar glaze with a spatula that has been dipped in warm water. On small pastry and delicate cakes, apply it with a pastry brush. Petits fours can be impaled on a fork and dipped completely into the glaze.

STRIPED PATTERN

Coat the cake with soft sugar glaze flavored with rum. Using a homemade pastry bag (see page 116), squeeze brown glaze (colored with cocoa) in parallel lines on the still-soft glaze. Draw a knife straight across the lines of glaze. With every line, reverse your direction (Figure 1).

PETIT FOURS

Coat round petits fours with sugar glaze and allow to dry. Then decorate with a marzipan blossom, red currant jelly, and melted chocolate (see page 116). Coat diamond-shaped petits fours with pink sugar glaze (add red food coloring), then decorate with strips of angelica, red currant jelly, and chocolate.

MARZIPAN ICING

To coat a round cake, cut a round paper stencil that is

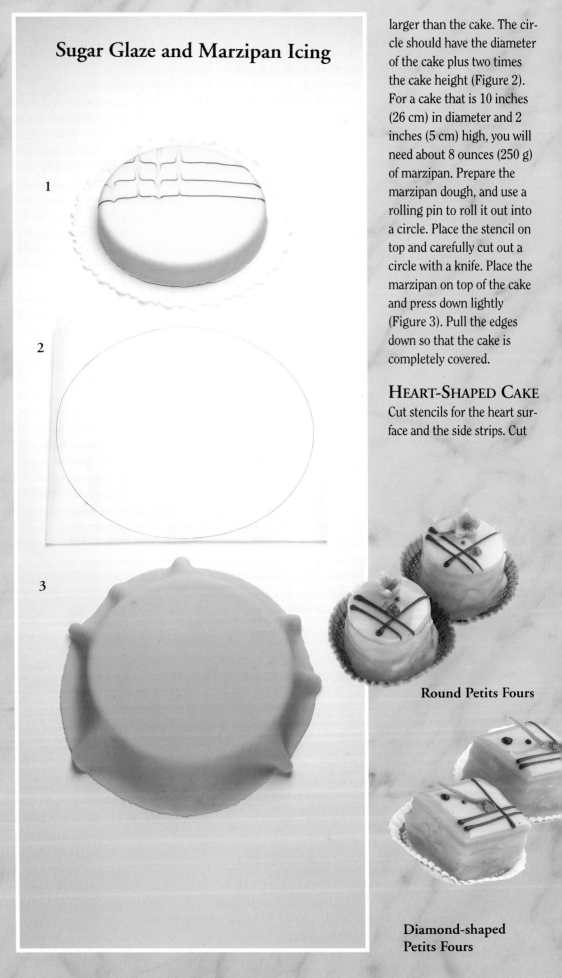

Sugar Glaze and Marzipan Icing

1

2

3

Round Petits Fours

Diamond-shaped Petits Fours

larger than the cake. The circle should have the diameter of the cake plus two times the cake height (Figure 2). For a cake that is 10 inches (26 cm) in diameter and 2 inches (5 cm) high, you will need about 8 ounces (250 g) of marzipan. Prepare the marzipan dough, and use a rolling pin to roll it out into a circle. Place the stencil on top and carefully cut out a circle with a knife. Place the marzipan on top of the cake and press down lightly (Figure 3). Pull the edges down so that the cake is completely covered.

HEART-SHAPED CAKE

Cut stencils for the heart surface and the side strips. Cut

Heart Cake

**Round Cake
With Striped Pattern**

**Round Cake
With Fan Pattern**

out both shapes from rolled-out marzipan. Place the top on the cake. Then place the long side strip around the edges, press it down, and join all edges. Lay another marzipan heart on top and decorate with silver pearls, sugar blossoms, marzipan cups (see page 123), and melted chocolate.

GLAZED FAN

Glaze the cake as described above (see Striped Pattern). This time arrange the lines in a fan shape. Decorate the cake with marzipan leaves (see page 122) and roses. To make a rose, start with a pear-shaped piece and thin circles. Press the circles onto the pear, starting at the top, and arrange them slightly overlapping from top to bottom. Cut the bottom off the middle piece and place the rose on the cake.

STRIPES

Make a striped pattern in the sugar glaze and decorate with marzipan cups .

Index